The Secret Sex of Books
Fiction 101

A Writer's Guide

© 2014 Deborah Greenspan

All rights reserved. No part of this publication may be reproduced or transmitted in any form or by any means electronic or mechanical, including photocopy, recording, or any information storage and retrieval system, without permission in writing from both the copyright owner and the publisher.

Requests for permission to make copies of any part of this work should be mailed to Permissions Department, Llumina Press, 7580 NW 5th St., Fort Lauderdale, FL 33318.

ISBN: 978-1-62550-0991 (PB)
ISBN: 978-1-62550-1004 (EB)

Printed in the United States of America by Llumina Press

The Secret Sex of Books
Fiction 101

A Writer's Guide

By Deborah Greenspan

Llumina Press

Dedication

This is dedicated to my children, the reason for everything I do. I'm so proud of you.

Acknowledgements

I've tried to sum up a lifetime's worth of knowledge, experience, training, and experimentation in these pages, all of it seasoned in the love of a few special people. I want to thank first, my mother, who always believed in me, and even though she's gone from this world, I think that somewhere, she's watching. I also have to thank my children—all grown up now—Cassandra for keeping me humble and Joe for seeing true and never failing to say what she thinks regardless of whether it will hurt or not. There is no better critic. I also want to thank my brother, Mike, and my sister-in-law, Diane, for helping me through some hard times and for being there when I needed them, and my niece, Shari, for loving me even when she forgets that she does. As for the learning that went into this book, the sources are everywhere and everyone. To all of you, my deepest gratitude.

Table of Contents

Prologue
Introduction
Why I wrote this book

STRUCTURE
The Art of Stories
The Storyteller Gene
Dream and Truth
Structure and How to See It
Structure of Feeling

BASIC TOOLKIT
The Breath of Life
Who is Your Reader?
POV
Theme
Arena or Setting
What is Your Main Conflict?
Resolution to the Main Conflict
Other Conflicts

TELLING THE STORY
Show. Don't Tell.
Plot
Subgoals and Plot Twists
Pivotal Plot Points
Defining Your Pivotal Plot Points
Plot Revisited
Beginning Your Story
The Middle of Your Story
The End of Your Story
Flashbacks

WHO IS IT ALL ABOUT?
Good and Evil
Identification and Person-ification
Who Is Your Protagonist?
Who or What Is Your Antagonist?
Love Interest
Supporting Characters
Agents and Sidekicks
Minor Characters
Character is Destiny
Analyze Plot and Character

GOD IS IN THE DETAILS
Dialogue
Tips on Dialogue
Grounding Dialogue
Setups and Payoffs
Creating Suspense
Foreshadowing
Writing Descriptions
Writing for Clarity
Clarity in Pivotal Scenes
Emotional Distance
Pacing and Momentum
On Being a God

PUTTING IT ALL TOGETHER
Write a Treatment
Analyze Your Treatment
Common Errors in English
Rules on Writing
Writing the First Draft
Analyze the Language
Analyze the Structure
Write the Rest
It's Done!

Prologue:

The Secret Sex of Books
Writer's Guides

By Deborah Greenspan

Welcome to *The Secret Sex of Books*. In this series, you will find multiple lessons designed to help you successfully write, publish, and market your book. These five helpful guides provide the following tools:

SS 101: FICTION – THE REPRODUCTION OF LIFE
Sixty lessons, discussions, workshops, and exercises that will help you:
- analyze your audience
- write with this audience in mind
- develop your characters
- develop your pivotal scenes
- prepare a treatment for your book
- analyze and edit your writing
- and much more

SS 102 – MEMOIR - BIRTH AND REBIRTH
Discussions, workshops, and exercises that will help you:
- analyze your audience
- write with this audience in mind
- develop your characters
- choose the scenes that matter most
- develop your pivotal scenes
- prepare a treatment for your book
- analyze and edit your writing
- and much more

SS 103: THE NON-FICTION FACTS OF LIFE
- narrowing your topic
- analyzing your market
- what's different about your approach?
- research
- incorporating what you learn
- and much more

SS 104: READING, WRITING, AND RE-CREATION
- children's books
- color or black and white
- picture book or WORKSHOP book
- who's your reader?
- illustrations
- and much more

SS 201: THE BIRDS AND THE BEES OF PUBLISHING AND MARKETING
- decide on how to publish the book
- find a publisher who provides the services you need
- maximize your available funds
- dissect and target your audience
- market and promote your book
- and much more

This series is written for writers and would-be writers who need help organizing and structuring a book, whether that's a novel, a memoir, a non-fiction book, or a children's picture book or chapter book. These guides are designed to help you climb out from under by minimizing your mistakes.

As a writer, you will learn new techniques, new ways of thinking, and new strategies on the long journey from idea to finished book to successful author. You can use the discussions in this book to polish and perfect a work in progress, or you can use it from the very beginning, before you put a word on paper.

Every chapter asks important questions and requires that you think through your book project thoroughly. The first four books focus on writing the book itself; the last one in the series on marketing and promoting it. If you want more than a copy of a book with your name on it to put on your bookshelf, you first need a book of which you can be proud, and then you need to let the world know about it.

Whether the purpose of your writing is to impart knowledge, share a vision, entertain, or leave a legacy for your grandchildren, this book is an indispensable tool for doing it right. It will save you time, ease you over the rough spots, help you make decisions, hone your skills, and enable you to write your book with the most likelihood of success.

The chapters in this book are interactive and cumulative. Many authors get the idea for a book in a kind of vision embracing the entire story—an inspiration or epiphany—and then start writing. If this happened to you, this book will help you clarify your ideas and create in reality the synergy between elements that characterized that first breathtaking idea, but if you haven't had that experience yet, don't despair; these discussions may help bring that moment on. As you bring your ideas to awareness, your mind will slowly sift the ore from around the gold and leave you with shining nuggets of understanding and power.

Descriptions combine techniques I learned from scriptwriting with those I've learned from writing novels, and I often use movies as well as books to show examples of the structures and techniques I'm explaining. Drama is drama, regardless of the medium, so while movies are limited by their visual nature, that same nature enables readers to see structures that may be less clearly delineated in a novel.

A novel is so closely interwoven, it's difficult to say do this and then do that. Every part, as in life, depends on every other part. Still, writing fiction requires that the novel and all its parts and processes be taken apart, so the reader can see how it's put together. Although you may have read other books about this, I guarantee that no one has done it quite like this.

At the back of this book are several forms designed to help you put your novel together. You can photocopy these, or (if you own the book) cut them out. They'll help you define your characters and your most important scenes.

These lessons shouldn't be rushed. You can think through and do the exercises or save them for another day, but you should set up a notebook and keep notes as you work through the chapters. The more you work with this material, the closer you'll get to turning your inspiration into a fully realized, professional work that can be published and marketed.

INTRODUCTION

Why *The Secret Sex of Books*?

In the beginning, there was the word, and the word was made flesh, or something like that. Although this idea from *Genesis* refers to the creation of the Universe by God, on a human level it may be seen to have other implications.

As humans, we cannot be separated from our ability to use language. While other animals do communicate, we have no idea how extensive their languages are, and we only know of one earthly species that writes down words. Other creatures may write their communiqués in DNA, for all we know, but only humans use symbols to stand for things.

The word is powerful. If we couldn't use words, it's quite possible our ability to think coherently and sequentially would be limited. We certainly could not have built the civilization we live in without this ability. We have books that are thousands of years old yet still influence our thinking today: *The Bible*, *The Koran*, the *Upanishads*, Aristotle's *Poetics* and many more. Wherever there is civilization, there are written words.

Everything that is made must first be written down. Want to build a building? You must draw up plans and instructions. Want to build a spaceship? Reports by the thousands will be generated. Want to explain how you came to be who you are? If it's possible to sum up a life at all, a memoir will do it best. Want to make others feel something you felt? Recreate the experience in words. Want to make others experience a place, time, life they've never known? Use fiction. You might argue that movies do it just as well, but every movie starts with a screenplay, which is written down. The written word is a way to recreate some portion of ourselves and our knowledge.

The act of creating a book can be likened to the act of creating a baby: It takes a long time. The brain of the mother (author) is inspired by an idea and proceeds to build upon that idea. At certain points in the process, the embryo will seem to be growing the wrong way and parts of it will be reabsorbed (rewritten) so that building can begin again. In a similar way, cell by cell, layer by layer, over time, the embryonic book will grow finer and finer until it's finished and perfect.

Then comes the labor involved in publishing (bringing it into the world) and the hands-on parenting required to give it legs (also known as marketing).

An idea comes to us, inspires us, and we begin to write—our purpose to reproduce that idea in a form that will allow us to share it with other humans. If we do it right, our "baby" will take its place in the world.

Is this just a metaphor? Or do books really have some kind of quasi-life that is all their own? Are good books written according to rules applied by a writer to paper, or are they something organic, inspired by mind and brought to birth by the labor of the author? Since this is *The Secret Sex of Books*, I believe the latter. I hope that in working through these lessons and workshops, you will also begin to understand the organic wholeness of a well-written book, and learn how to pull one together.

And what do books have to do with sex? Are the paperbacks having title-to-title contact with the hardcovers in the aisles of the bookstore? Are stacks of books getting it on in some massive literary orgy? Could the two books pressed up against each other in the corner be having more fun than we imagine? Can we even contemplate what might be going on in the library?

No. Let's not go there. Books don't have sex with each other, or gender, for that matter, so what's this secret sex of books about? It's true that many books are about sex or involve sex in some way, but we're not talking about content. Why then the secret sex of books?

When it comes down to it, this is more about people than it is about books. There's a reason why some books "work," and others don't. Yes, there's all that stuff about plot, character, style, rising action, voice, dramatic moment, scene, mood, pace, momentum, fatal flaws, saving graces, theme, character arc etc., and all of this matters, but at rock bottom, the most important thing about books is that people read them, and the most basic "part" of a book is its structure. You could almost call it its soul, and that's what this book is about.

I first started thinking about this when I learned in grade school that works of fiction reach a climax. I thought it was a strange word. We rarely encounter it, especially when we're ten years old. I was an avid reader even then, however, and the word fascinated me. Climax. Our textbooks defined it as "the resolution of the plot," which told me little. It wasn't until years later that I started to hone in on what that really meant.

We hardly ever talk about climaxes except when discussing sex and stories. Movies have climaxes; books have climaxes; musical pieces all reach for a climax; our lives can achieve a climax, even diseases have climaxes. I wouldn't be surprised if the word is used to describe some conclusive moment in higher mathematics too. However, the most common use of the word has to do with sex, although we usually call it orgasm or coming. Another strange word, which we'll talk about later.

Of course, no book is complete without a climax. It may be cold and dry as in a scholarly dissertation, but it's there nevertheless. It's the point where everything spoken of earlier comes together. It's the culmination of all that went before, the summit of the mountain already climbed, and that's what this book is about.

Along with structure and climax, this book is about people. People write and read books. While we can write about Martians or other alien species, other worlds, physics, spirituality, divinity, anger, food, politics, poison, psychology, and anything else we can dream up, the only ones reading our books are other humans. It's the humanness of the reader (and the writer) that shapes the book, the humanness of the writer (and the reader) that determines its structure.

Ultimately, *The Secret Sex of Books* is about love and about loving. Art is, after all, related to reality, and our writing reveals who we are as people. We write about what we know or what we imagine. We create characters who become real to us, and in the words of the book, we reveal who we are. Readers, for their part, reveal themselves in their choices. Do they only read murder mysteries? Do they prefer historical fiction? Our choices as both writer and reader reveal who we are, what we like, what interests us, but it's in the structure of the book, the secret soul of the book, that we reveal how we relate to others and let the world know how we love.

There are many structures in a book. There's the plot structure, the structure of feeling, the character arc, and all these structures are about the relationship of one part to another and the changing of this organization over time. The soul of the book is in the most basic structure: the writer's relationship to the reader and how it's revealed in the course of the story.

Sex, life, love, and how it's turned into art. That's what this book is about.

Why I Wrote this Book

I wanted to be a writer since I was ten, and I wrote my first poem (it was about Mars for some reason). I hoped that someday I would be smart enough, wise enough, and lucky enough to be able to write something that would be of value to other humans.

I started practicing very young, writing terrible stories and awful, long treatises on my views on reality. I learned a lot from these initial forays into the art of writing, but not enough. I had so much to learn and no one to teach me, so in the end, I learned everything I know from firsthand experience—from mistakes as well as successes.

My first inkling that I might be getting somewhere came in my mid-twenties when I took a playwriting class. The play I wrote was funny, and everyone laughed in all the right places. This inspired me to move forward with a screenplay. Over the course of ten years, I rewrote this script every time I took it out of the closet and reread it. After many years and many rewrites, it was actually good and opened some doors for me to write other screenplays and video scripts (which I did for a living after getting my Masters in Communication at the age of forty-five).

While working as a freelance writer, I finished several screenplays and turned four of them into books. It turned out that a screenplay is a pretty good structure on which to base a book. Another book began as a book, inspired by an experience I had at the age of sixteen.

After I got my Masters, I taught some college classes in screenwriting and in public speaking, but the truth is, most of my writing credentials come from the school of hard knocks. From trial and error. From studying the work of all kinds of writers, breaking down what I saw, mimicking techniques, and seeing if the result was good.

After I graduated college, I soon started my own publishing business and became editor and mentor to many, many writers. In fourteen years, we've published over 2300 books, so I have a lot of experience in not only writing, but in publishing as well.

I like the way I learned; it was right for me. However, if I had it to do over again, I might think twice. Instead of reinventing the wheel, I would go to college and let the professors lead me through the knowledge that is already there. Instead of reading novels to learn how writers do it, I would have read more books about writing, books like this one. That way I would have reached my goal much younger. In fact, if I had done it that way, I might have been the famous writer I'd always dreamed of being.

On the other hand, I wonder what, if anything, I would have written about. Had I lived such a life, I would certainly not be me, and any book I wrote would not be a book that I would write.

A college professor once described me as an "original thinker," and I think she was right. It's entirely because I lived an authentic and original life, so no matter how much I might have gained by living more conventionally, I would not exchange my life or the knowledge and understanding gained from it for anything at all.

That said, it's my pleasure to be able to share what I've learned along my journey with other writers.

STRUCTURE

WORKSHOP 1

THE ART OF STORIES

Long ago, I used to draw, as well as write. I took up this occupation when my oldest daughter was an infant because I was going crazy waiting on her all day. I needed something interesting to keep me busy. Writing took too much concentration and didn't lend itself to frequent interruptions, but art was ideal. My first attempt was a portrait of the baby in pastels. It was to be a gift for my mother, and as it progressed from an approximation of a baby to a creditable baby to an actual portrait, I learned a great deal about myself and about art in general.

One of the most important lessons was that art requires a good eye. You can't draw it if you can't see it clearly. This is true no matter what your medium. Whether you paint in pastels or words, you cannot accurately portray what you cannot accurately see. Like the stroke of the chalk on paper, words either add to or detract from the description of truth, and one of the most frequent errors that writers make is in using the wrong word—a word that approximates, but doesn't quite catch their exact meaning. Very often, the reason is they haven't imagined their story clearly enough to "see" the right word. Being a good observer is crucial.

Besides teaching me to see more clearly, pastels taught me about what I call the "work" of art. Being creative and letting the impulse flow from muse to fingertips is great, but usually there is a stop along the way known as "technique" or work. Art is a construction project. To create a pastel painting, we need paper, chalks, light, pencils, erasers, a subject, an inspiration, and the willingness to spend as many hours, days, or weeks as it takes to turn that inspiration into reality. In this art, we use color, line, and texture; we compare this shadow against that to see degrees of light and shade. We compare the length of this line against that to see form.

Written works are similarly constructed, but instead of physical colors and papers, our tools are words, grammar, computers, keyboards, imagination, inspiration, and a willingness to work long and hard to get our book out of our heads and into the world. We construct our book using theme, motive, character, dialogue, plot, subplot, and climax. We weave emotion and action into the picture and use words to illustrate our thoughts. Although we might like the whole thing to flow from mind to matter without effort, that isn't usually what happens.

I learned one more really important lesson from my artwork—that the more you work on it, the better it gets. At one point, I was pretty happy with my efforts. The baby looked like a baby; the colors were beautiful. But it bothered me that it didn't quite look like MY baby, so I kept at it. I must have erased that little face and reworked it fifteen times. It took weeks. And then, there it was: my own baby girl on the paper. It was something I had never done before, and it was miraculous. Translated to the art of writing, it comes down to that old adage: writing is rewriting.

Writing, painting, sculpture, music—it doesn't really matter. In art, as in life, God is in the details. If you want your work to progress from an approximation to an incisive illustration of truth as you see it, you have to see clearly, master your tools, and work on it until it shines.

Observation Exercises:

1) Take out a sheet of paper and a pencil and copy your foot. Maybe you're not an artist, but this exercise is not meant to train eye-hand coordination. It's meant to help you learn to see more clearly. Before you even begin to draw, study your foot carefully. Study the way light hits the foot. Look at the shadows and the highlights. Look at how the color changes depending on the light. Examine the form. See how one curve leads into another. How the length of one line measures up against another. Look at the shape of the nails. Try to see past what you've always seen to what is actually there before trying to draw what you see. After it's done, erase whatever's not right and draw it over.

2) Write a paragraph describing the taste of chocolate. After you've written it, get a chocolate kiss. Study it carefully. Look at the shape. See how the foil winds around the tip, and how the paper label emerges from the foil. Tug on the paper and observe how it's attached or not attached to the wrapper. Bring the kiss to your nose and inhale. Think about the aroma and the words that describe that smell as accurately as possible. Open the wrapper slowly and smell again. Is the odor stronger now? Are there any words you might add to your

description? Lick the chocolate, but don't eat it. How does the taste add to the experience? Touch it with your tongue again. Slowly, let it melt in your mouth. Enjoy it fully, rapturously. Examine the texture, the taste, and the aroma at various stages of enjoyment. Try to bring words to your mind that you might not have used before to describe chocolate. Also examine your feelings as you go through the experience. See how you feel when the chocolate is gone. Now, rewrite the paragraph.

WORKSHOP 2

THE STORYTELLER GENE

We live in stories. We create stories to explain our place in the world, the events that happen to us, and the things we do. Everyone is a storyteller, if only to themselves. For example, a girl bumps into a guy in a store. In an instant, as she looks at him, she creates a whole story about him of which she may or may not be aware. The story could feature him as a thief waiting for her to give him a chance to get at her purse. Her response is to hold it tighter to her body. Or if the man is attractive to her, the story could be about love and marriage. In that event, she might smile or say something, or if she's shy, she might do nothing, hoping he'll take the initiative.

Stories are useful because they help us frame reality into a coherent system. Reality is a seething mass of impressions: sounds, sights, tastes, smells, and touches. In addition, we have an inner reality that is a boiling cauldron of ideas, impressions, fears, anxieties, desires, and needs. To make sense of it, we create structures. We have weekends and holidays that help us structure our days. We eat breakfast when we get up, lunch in the middle of the day, and dinner in the evening, and can anchor ourselves around those times. Even if our day is one long, confusing puzzle from beginning to end, we know we have to eat. We have relatives who define our place in our families, and social groups who define our place in society. We go to church or temple, and this helps us understand our position relative to God and the divine. We fall in love, changing all our other relationships in the process, and learn more about who we are and what we want. We buy things because they help us define who we are. We wear black rather than white. We like flashy jewelry, or we don't. We choose the things that we like—from cars to houses to cups—and these things tell us who we are. Our jobs serve a similar purpose. If you've ever been fired, or had to suddenly leave a job, then you know how much that job served to define your place in reality. We take political positions or ignore the whole process. We read certain types of books and not others. All these are things that help us feel safe and comfortable in the world. Creating stories serves the same purpose.

But how do we connect all these disparate desires, needs, people, jobs, and choices that define who we are? It's simple, and we often do it without conscious thought: We create relationships, and then fill in the story structure that supports those relationships. For example, let's say I live in a house with my older husband, who is sick, and I take care of him every day. I take him to the doctor and feed him at night, but I'm not very happy about it; I chafe at the limits it puts on my personal freedom. We know that story. It can end in a murder or a mercy killing. Perhaps a man will be involved. Now, that doesn't mean that I'm going to *do* anything like that. I'm not going to allow my sick husband to die. In fact, I'll probably do a better job of taking care of him than I would have done had the story not crossed my mind. This is because I feel guilty for it even flitting across my consciousness.

Another example: Every day, I go to work at the same old job, which I hate. I don't know why I do it. Perhaps

I'm afraid of change. Or maybe it's because I don't know how to do anything else. Or maybe it's because I like the people I work with, even though I don't like the job. Maybe I have a crush on the boss. Or maybe I think I might meet someone there someday. All these are stories. They could all be true, or they could all be false. And it really doesn't matter. The stories help me continue to bring in the money necessary to pay the rent and eat.

If I'm a creative storyteller, I may be able to connect the dots of all these stories and make them into a single story that keeps me going: She didn't like her job, but she knew it was just a stepping-stone to something much finer...

Creating stories is a wholly human process serving various purposes:
1. They help us learn about ourselves.
2. They help us learn about each other and the world.
3. They help us do the things we have to do, even when we don't want to.
4. They give us pleasure.
5. They help us plan for the future, imagining different outcomes to different plots we might set in motion.

So it is within us all to be storytellers. It's a natural human talent to tell stories of varying degrees of complexity. It is a biological ability seated in the human genome. And while some of us may have more developed storytelling skills than others, it's nothing that cannot be developed, in the same way that we can learn to play the guitar or paint a picture. While we may not be Michelangelo or Rembrandt, that doesn't mean we can't create stories that will make us happy and provide enjoyment to other people.

What does it take to develop your storytelling ability?

Storytellers have certain traits. They:

1. Are able to see clearly
2. Understand that they are writing for an audience as well as themselves.
3. Are able to communicate clearly and grammatically
4. Are able to rewrite as often as necessary
5. Have a clear understanding of the sexual nature of fiction
6. Are disciplined
7. Are able to persevere

Exercise:

Open your notebook and as quickly as you can, jot down the basic storyline to as many stories as come to mind.

If nothing comes to mind, use these groups of ideas to help you get started:

Home
Alone
Winter
Visitor

Cruise ship
Friends
Port of call

Accident

Another planet
Useful resources
Indigenous life
Idealist

Foreign country
Estranged couple
Lost
Dead body

House
Teenager
Terrible loss
Miracle

WORKSHOP 3
THE DREAM AND THE TRUTH

The writer of fiction is essentially constructing (or reproducing) a dream in which the reader can get lost for a time. This dream involves the reader's emotions and judgment, so that he or she actually participates in the dream. While reading your story, the dream becomes the reader's, and whatever you don't state will be filled in by his or her mind.

This dream-like construction differs from real dreams in one very substantial way: although the fictional dream can be about any place, any time, any reality, it cannot flit from here to there without reason and cause. Although we can fly without wings in both dreams and fiction, in fiction, we need to explain how this is possible. If it's some new sci-fi technology, we want to have some idea of the reasoning behind it. If it's just that the fantasy world we've created includes flying, we have to see the consistency of this truth throughout that world. You can't just throw it in without it changing the world you've created. For example, if you created a world in which people fly, there would be problems maintaining borders between nations. Maybe in this world, nations wouldn't exist. This type of thing must be thought through, so that the fantasy feels real at every level of sensation and thought.

Although fiction is an invented story about invented people; in reality, fiction is all about truth. Although we may create the most outlandish circumstances, our characters must ring true. They must follow their own nature; they must speak the way real people speak. They must be true to themselves, whoever they are. Even if they are completely alien, they have to be true to that alienness.

In other words, you cannot have a character who is cheap and stingy hand twenty dollars to a beggar because that bill changing hands is necessary to the advancement of the plot. Bits of untruth like this jar the reader and interrupt the fictional dream, making the reader wonder if you have any idea what you're doing. Consistency and truth in character, setting, and action enable the reader to stay within the dream and follow it to its conclusion. Anything that makes the reader look up from the book and say, "that doesn't make sense," does not belong.

In addition, there are elements that do belong. Details that lend substance to the world you've created need to be included. In a world of flying beings, this might be loose, fluttery clothes that help us see the wind under their wings. The dark world of the homeless, on the other hand, might be enlivened with odors and dust. You could illustrate solitude by using barren, cold environments. Or you could do just the opposite and show how alone a character is by juxtaposing crowds of laughing people.

Exercises:

What are the most extraordinary elements of your story? Characters? Plot? Setting?

Explain how you'll make these elements real and

believable. Think of the details that impart depth and dimension, and develop them fully. Visualize the settings and write down keywords that will help you evoke those settings. Hear the sounds of the world and the speech of your characters. Breathe in the scents, taste the foods and the kisses, and touch the objects that exist in this dream. If you can do this, you will be able to share these sensations with your readers, and make your fictional reality real.

WORKSHOP 4

STRUCTURE – HOW TO SEE IT

Books are frequently long and involved. Whole worlds are created inside them, and it's not always easy to see the framework on which the story is laid. We see the plot, the characters, the locale. We experience the mood, and the rising tension. We see the trees rustling in the wind as described, and the rich contrast of the blue door under the yellow roses. But the structure evades us.

Structure is largely invisible. It's not on the page. You can't point to a passage in the book and say, "look, here's the structure." While we know what we're talking about when we discuss the structure of a house or a cold, the structures of books are more obscure.

The house is built on wood or steel beams laid out on a foundation or slab in patterns of rooms. We can see where the electricity will run in the walls and lead to steel boxes that will end neatly as wall outlets. We see where the piping will go that leads to the bathrooms and kitchen. We can see the framing of the windows and doors, and we can see the roof joists and the plywood base of the roof. It's all there, and if we observe the house before all this is covered up, we'll know it deeply.

However, what we won't see, unless we're aware of the structure is how it's constructed over time. We won't see how the concrete is poured before the carpenters arrive on the scene. We won't see that the electricians and plumbers will do their work before the drywall can be nailed to the beams and the plastering and painting done. We won't see how the roof will be installed before the plaster and paint. This structure, the work done over time, is invisible, but is an intrinsic part of the house.

A cold has a structure over time too. It begins with a tickle or scratchiness at the back of the throat and progresses through various stages including sore throat, one stuffy nostril, and then the other. Fever rises from the start, reaches a climax and begins to fall more rapidly than it rose.

Everything that exists has structure. Everything. From a rock to a war, there is a structure. We may not see the chain of events and people that structure a war until it's long over and the historians get their hands on it, but it's there. A series of events, characters with power, people willing to participate, a dispute...

Relationships have structure. Structure could actually be defined as the relationship or organization between components over time. Relationships *are* structure. Without relationship, there is no structure. It's the relationship between this man, this woman, and this child that makes three separate people into a family. It's the relationship between the CEO of a company, the workers, and the customers that enables the company to work and make money.

If you've ever felt forced to play a role in some relationship, you have observed firsthand, the power of the structure. The structure is the soul of the story, whether that story occurs in real time in our lives, on a movie screen, or in the pages of a book.

Some have compared the structure of a story, especially in movie form, to a roller coaster with twists and turns, low points and high points, and this can help us see the structure. It's easy to compare rising action to the rise of the track, and to see how a roller coaster moving in time has a structure that defines the ride.

For a writer, it can help to envision your story in terms of ups and downs, twists and turns, but I think it leaves a lot to be desired. The structure of books is far more complex while, at the same time, being amazingly simple. Each character has his or her own internal ride; there's a structure to the ride itself (the plot), and there's also a structure to the feelings experienced by the reader. All these structures are built upon the basic structure, which is the structure of the relationship between writer and reader. All these structures winding around each other create the book.

I'll tell you a secret. Everything in art is about human sexuality. We like to pretend that it's not, that art is above all that, but on this subject we lie to ourselves all the time. The sexual act is the defining moment of our lives. We are created in that moment, and it's our drive to reproduce ourselves in flesh or in some other way that defines how we live.

Sexuality propels us toward awareness, and love or lust is the cause of most of our happiness and sorrow. Because of this—the all-pervasive nature of our sexuality—I have found that the easiest way to understand a scene, an act, or a story is to think of it in those terms. The structure of the sexual encounter is the structure on which our stories are built.

We could break it down like this: In the beginning, we meet someone. We explore who they are and ourselves in relation to them. We pull apart and anticipate our next meeting. We meet again. The sense of urgency begins to rise. We talk more deeply of who we are. Maybe something happens to make us wonder if this could ever work. We have our moments of doubt and yet move forward. We kiss.

The motion of in and out has begun long before the two actually enter into a sexual act, but when they do, the act itself is advance, withdraw, move forward, retreat, reach for ecstasy, back off. The pace quickens as these two opposing forces meet more and more frequently until finally, events climax and we either fall into loving arms and whisper sweet nothings or not.

Please understand that this is not a description of a particular scene; it is a metaphor graphically illustrating the *structure* of the scene. In fact, it illustrates the structure of all scenes, all acts, and all stories. Beneath all art, is this structure.

Books, like plays and movies, usually have three to five acts. We do not call them acts in books and they may not be as clearly cut as they are on stage. However, the parts of a novel, the acts, are very similar to those in the theater. There is Act I (the beginning) in which the characters are introduced, the conflict is established and the plot is initiated. (They meet, they explore each other; they kiss.) Then there is the second Act (the middle) in which the story takes off, obstacles are overcome, events begin to merge and trouble brews. (This is the act itself, where we begin to overcome obstacles as every motion forward meets with opposition. The pace begins to quicken until the opposing forces hover on the brink of their final showdown.) In the third Act, there is no escape. The characters are caught in the web of events and must follow through to the climax. (They cannot walk away until it's over.)

Just as paragraphs are made of sentences, stories are made up of acts, and acts are made up of scenes. And just as sentences have subjects, verbs and objects, scenes have characters, actions and objectives. There is a "grammar" to scene construction that is not so different in its way from the grammar of language itself. In every scene, there is a beginning, a middle, and an end. There is order, organization, relationship, and logic. Words are put together in a sentence to convey an idea. Sentences are then ordered into paragraphs to communicate a larger idea. And so on. The micro-universe of the word is joined with other word-universes to convey more and more complex ideas in the same way that atoms join to atoms to create the entire symphony of existence. Words must be put together in sentences so that ambiguity, repetition, and illogic are avoided. Scenes must also avoid these hazards to build the larger units of acts.

A character in action always has an objective, a motivation, a reason why he's in the scene at all. If there is no objective, there's no reason for the character to be on stage. So when writing a scene, it follows that the first thing you must define is why you're writing it. What is its purpose? Why does this particular scene exist? Is it to show us who the character is? Is it to advance the plot in some way? Is the scene necessary to show or solve a problem, develop character, setup or payoff a situation? All of these are legitimate purposes for a scene, and if it can do double or triple-duty by realizing more than one of these purposes, then it is an even stronger scene.

The Grammar of Scenes

Scenes have grammar. Each scene has a beginning, a middle, and an end, meaning that it will introduce the character, show the character in action, and then reach a conclusion of some type. It will be structured like the sexual act in microcosm. There will be a happy or an unhappy conclusion. (They whisper sweet nothings or they split apart).

So now, understanding the structure of scene, act and story, we can go ahead to create a scene. Let's say our scene is about a man who wants a woman he'll never have. The purpose of the scene in our story is to show why this man, the antagonist, hates the hero so much. It also shows us what kind of man he is. (In this scene, he is pursuing the love interest.) She has a purpose in this scene too: to get away from him.

Now that we know all that, we have to set the scene. Where and when does the action take place? Our characters live in the future in an underground habitat established before they were born. Specifically, the action takes place in Evie's cubicle.

> One day, he followed her back to her cubicle and opened the door, which was never locked, to find her getting undressed. Her back was toward him and his breath caught as she peeled off the navy jumpsuit, revealing the slender curves of her back and buttocks. As she turned toward the shower—her long,

blonde hair swinging—she saw him in the doorway and froze.

Morgan enjoyed the moment. He admired her breasts and belly, even the look of shock on her face. He stepped forward, crossing the eight feet between them, and reached out. Evie whirled out of reach, slamming the door of the bathroom in his face.

Angry now, Morgan turned the handle and pushed on the door. He was strong and wiry, and she was just fourteen, so it didn't take long for him to push it back far enough to get a hand inside. The pain as a pair of nail scissors went into his hand was unbearable, but he grunted in agony and kept pushing. This wasn't about sex anymore. Now it was about control. He would have her. She would be his.

And Morgan's will might have made it so, except that Evie was just as determined that he would not have her, that she would not be his. She pulled the scissors out of his hand and stabbed him again, and this time Morgan couldn't do anything but withdraw his arm. Evie slammed the door closed and locked it.

Swearing, he opened her tiny closet, pulling out a shirt and wrapping his arm and hand. The pain lessened slightly and blood stopped pouring out. Morgan sat down on the bed to get his breath.

"You'd better get out of here," Evie said from behind the door.

"You can't stay in there forever."

"Get out of here, John, or I won't be responsible for what happens to you."

Morgan laughed. "What happens to me?"

There was silence for several minutes. Then there was a knock on the door. Morgan didn't know what to do. There was blood everywhere. Evie was locked in the bathroom. The knock came again, and then the voice of Jersey Lipton.

"Evie! Evie, what the hell is going on in there? There's talcum powder pouring out of the vents. Is everything all right?"

Morgan cringed. She'd dumped powder into the air vent and it was flooding the hall. Pulling his dignity like a robe around him, he got up, opened the door and walked out, pushing past Lipton and disappearing around the corner.

This scene can be broken down into its parts: the **beginning**, in which the scene is set. We see that John Morgan has stepped into her room and is admiring her nakedness. Structurally, this is the prelude to the act, or it can be seen as the inciting event. It's the setup for the scene that is about to take place. We know what he's planning. The beginning ends as Morgan steps forward and reaches out to touch her. Structurally, this is the kiss even though he doesn't even get close.

We are now committed to the action, and the **middle** of the scene begins. Structurally, this is the sexual act itself. The action involves two opposing forces, both trying to meet their own objectives and reach their own climax. These have changed a bit since the scene began. Evie began the scene wanting to take a shower; now she has to escape the attentions of a would-be rapist. There is a push and pull, a motion forward and back in the action itself. Morgan pushes the door open; Evie responds by thrusting a pair of scissors into his hand; Morgan continues to push and she does it again. Morgan retreats. Evie warns him to get out. Morgan laughs.

The third part of the scene, the **end**, begins in the actual climax. This takes place in the moment when Jersey Lipton knocks on the door and reveals that Evie has created a storm of talcum powder in the hallway. This is the moment when all is revealed, when both parties are completely exposed. In this moment, they meet and they know each other, even though in this case that meeting is the very antithesis of coming together. Then the action slacks off. Morgan pushes past Lipton and disappears down the hall. No doubt to nurse his disappointment and anger.

WORKSHOP 5

STRUCTURE OF FEELING

In a work of fiction, readers are open systems that will be changed by the story. They are active participants, and the author must always be aware of this presence. The whole story is created for this reader; all this work done so that the reader will go through the experience as designed by the author. If we see the sexual act behind the structure of fiction, we can begin to see that the relationship between the writer and reader also follows this pattern. In essence, you, the writer, are enjoying a serious, deeply committed relationship with your reader. While no actual physical contact is involved, the relationship is still sexual in nature. It can be manipulative, overpowering, arrogant, joyous, artful, sensual, tender, sensitive, or loving.

As the writer, you can be clumsy with the reader's feelings, or you can be gentle. You can be seductive or brazen. A great writer may be all these things at different times, but will always treat his reader with respect and love, setting the scene, preparing his lover for what is to come, and oh, so sensitively, bringing him to the final moment. As the writer, it's up to you to determine how your reader feels at any given moment, and while a little awkwardness at first can be endearing, clumsiness rarely is. While seduction can be powerful, few will be seduced by a fake. I believe that great lovers make great writers and probably vice versa as well.

Primarily, as we've already said, fiction is an experience. We want our readers to actively participate by experiencing certain feelings. We want them to hate the antagonist, to love the hero, to wish the girl success in capturing the hero's heart, to desire the hero or the girl for themselves, as well as for each other, to feel suspense and fear when the conflict reaches its crescendo, and to feel relief and joy when it's all over. If someone important dies, we want the reader to cry. We want the reader to feel curious at first and move toward feeling more involved every moment because the minute we lose the reader's involvement, he puts down the book, and our seduction is a failure.

Within the pages of a book, screenplay, or theatrical performance is a structure that few besides seasoned writers recognize or understand. Some call it the structure of feeling. It is the invisible structure of emotional ups and downs, twists and turns, that the reader is going through at any given time. You've seen how plot points can be likened to the sexual act itself or to a car on a roller coaster. The track of the roller coaster is also a good way to envision the feelings of the audience. First, there's the exciting moments when it all begins, when that long chain pulls us up to the top before letting us go and setting the ride in motion. You could compare this to the setup or the first chapter of a book in which we get to know the characters and their relationships and see the plot take off.

During this first rise toward the first drop off, the reader should be curious and should anticipate the coming action. We create these feelings in him; make him curious by leaving out certain information about the characters and their relationships. These unanswered questions get him thinking about what will happen.

Why did she walk out on the hero? Why is the boy so scared of his mother? Who is that fat man? How does he figure into all this?

At the very top of this first rise (in our other metaphor) is the kiss—the commitment that begins the action. Now the ride begins in earnest as the reader is hurled around this curve or that bend, made to feel every emotion we can draw from him. Each upslope arouses his curiosity and draws him toward the dangerous edge of another drop off, and as he screams down the down slope, he may expect that this is the end. But it's not; instead of riding into the gate, there's another climb and another drop off. Thus it continues until we pull him up that last slope, the most frightening one of all, and finally deliver him safely to the end of the ride.

Can you imagine a roller coaster that meandered along without all the ups and downs? That would be a boring ride. In the same way, a flat structure of feeling in a book will bore its readers. There's a scene in *Parenthood*, starring Steve Martin, which illustrates this perfectly. The grandmother says something like, "Some people like to go on the merry-go-round, but that's boring. It just goes around and around. I like the roller coaster." Later on, as Steve watches his son tear apart the school play, the room around him begins to rise and fall, like a roller coaster. At first, he's afraid, but then he gets it, and he laughs. It is the purpose of your book to take your reader on a ride they won't forget.

Here are some feelings that you might elicit from the reader:

POSITIVE FEELINGS:
    Ecstasy
    Thrill
    Joy
    Excitement
    Delight
    Interest
    Boredom

NEGATIVE FEELINGS:
    Grief
    Sadness
    Terror
    Fright
    Anxiety
    Interest
    Boredom

You can make the reader feel good or make him feel bad, or you can just try to keep him interested. You never want him to descend to boredom. If that happens, you've lost him.

THE BASIC TOOLKIT

Copyright 2011 Cassandra Skevis

WORKSHOP 6

TAKING IT APART

It all starts with a moment—the moment when a single idea, a simple thought like "truth in fiction," fires off a series of neurons that light up the entire brain. In that moment, a concept arises, whole and complete: an epiphany. You want to live in it forever, never return to the world of things, but you have no choice. You're a writer—an artist—and so must take this perfect moment, dissect it, find out what its parts are, and then put it back together in a way that exposes the moment in all its fullness and glory.

That's how books often begin: with an inspiration. The inspiration is like a waking dream in which all the parts are there, even if you can't sort them out in the brightness of the flash. In that moment, your mind has put it all together and taken a sort of picture that's stored in your subconscious. The picture is there, and it's complete. It's like a photo to be developed. If you were a visual artist, you might actually see this image in your mind's eye and transfer it to canvas or paper. It's harder to take apart an inspiration and write a book, but if you can test what you put on paper against the photo in your mind, and if you work at it hard enough, eventually, you will succeed.

If you're a writer of non-fiction, you may find that it will take research to discover all the parts and where they belong in the text. Nevertheless, everything you will discover is already implied in the inspiration. It includes not only your questions but your conclusions as well. You'll just need to dig up the materials that confirm what you already know. Sometimes, you'll discover facts that alter your original vision, but if you're a true artist, you will never let dogma (even the dogma of your original beliefs) stop you from revealing the truth.

For writers of fiction and filmmakers, it's even more difficult: the inspiration includes transformations over time, thoughts, characters, motivations, sequential actions, obstacles, a climax, and denouement. A fictional story is the most complex and takes the most work to develop. Your purpose will be to examine that inspiration from every angle, digging it out from under the dross of ordinary existence, and revealing the light beneath, the same light that drove you to start this project. While taking apart your vision, you will discover new things about yourself and others. Sometimes, you'll get discouraged and tired of the project, but sometimes you'll feel inspired and powerful. Just remember, your purpose as an artist is to take apart your inspiration and put it back together in words. Only in this way will be you able to share your truth with the world.

As you begin, keep this in mind: There are no wrong answers. There are no right answers. There are only *your* answers. So be honest; dig deep for your own truth. And use a pencil.

Writing Exercise:

Think of the experience of chocolate as if it were an inspiration. Take it apart and then put it back together.

Write down the elements that make up the chocolate experience: how it looks, how it smells, how it feels to unwrap it, how it tastes, how it feels when it's gone. Break down the experience into separate experiences. Then write a short sensual paragraph about eating chocolate. Make it real enough that someone reading it would want to go out and get a piece.

When it's finished, have a friend read it and see if it makes them want to get a piece of chocolate. Be sure and have a chocolate kiss for them to enjoy when they're done.

WORKSHOP 7

THE BREATH OF LIFE

As we've already discussed, at the core of every story is a central moment—what some call the dramatic moment. This is the inspiration, the breath of life that begot the story and started you on this path. It's the moment it all came together in your head, and you went, "That's it!" (Or even "Eureka!") It may have left behind an idea, a scene, a smell, a character, an event, a thought. It could be anything, but whatever it is, it is the central point about which everything else in the novel spins. It's the experience that prompted you to get a pen and paper and start writing. Remembering that central moment is important because, if you are aware of it, you can use it to structure your novel.

If you cannot remember the image or thought that urged you onto this path, perhaps your idea is not yet fully defined and will be become clearer as you get into the writing. This happened with one book I wrote, *Mirror, Mirror*. It started out as a true story based on the life of a friend whose bi-polar son committed suicide. Because it was her story, there was no inspirational moment, but as I worked on it, as it flowed through and began to emerge from the well of my subconscious, an image surfaced of this boy being in love. From there, the story, which had limped along until then, began to write itself.

In another case, my moment came in a dream. I saw the main character tending a garden and spores falling from the sky. When I woke, I thought a lot about this dream, and slowly built around that moment, a wonderful science fiction trilogy called *Reconception*.

What was your inspiration or dramatic moment? If you're not sure, then write down whatever ideas came out of that moment. These are your first clues to untangling your story. Take each idea and try to flesh it out. Ask yourself questions.

What is it about your book that is universal? Is it about love, hate, God, relationships? Think about the theme. Play with ideas and see what comes up. If something takes your breath away for a moment, that's probably what you're looking for.

WORKSHOP 8

WHO IS YOUR READER?

Unlike humans, who are open biological systems taking the environment inside, using parts of it, and returning the rest to the surroundings, *stories* (if they're written down) are closed systems. They remain the same, no matter how many times they're told. (This is not true of oral fiction, which may change as the audience reacts to it.) However, even though written stories are closed systems, readers are open. This means readers must be considered part of the process because, while the story stays the same, the reader is changed by it. In fact, the main purpose of fiction is to move the reader in some way: to make him laugh, cry, scream with tension, fall in love, lose himself, and most of all, keep turning the pages.

Before you put pen to paper, you should have a clear picture of who is going to be reading your book. Is it for children, teenagers, women, mothers, men only, everyone? For example, there would be a tremendous difference between an erotic book written for women and one written for men. Even if it were the same story, the two audiences would demand completely different writing styles. Men's erotic material is far more graphic and uses words that women's erotica would avoid. Children's stories need to be written in simpler sentences with a modest vocabulary. Teen stories need to be up to date on slang and current trends in clothing and music. Books written for women tend to be about women, relationships, and love, while books written for everyone usually feature a man/hero in action. The more carefully you dig into the nature of your audience, the more clearly you'll be able to define your writing strategies.

Who is your reader? Narrow your definition as much as possible.

Visualize people who personify your reader. Is Aunt Harriet one of them? Your next-door neighbor? Your ex-girlfriend or boyfriend? Give specific examples of people you know who would pick up your book in a bookstore or library and take it home to read. If you can't visualize these people, go through magazines and find pictures that embody them.

Now that you know who your readers are, how will you reach them? What about your book will appeal to them and why? Is it writing style, length of book, type of story, genre? Make a list of the ways your book will appeal to your reader.

The better you define this "person," the better your book will relate to him/her.

WORKSHOP 9

POINT OF VIEW

Someone is telling your story. It can be you, or it can be a character within the story. There are essentially two easily accessible POV techniques: limited third person omniscient or first person. There are other points of view, but it's inadvisable for you to try them. For instance, do not attempt to tell a story in the second person (me talking to you). This may work in nonfiction, but it won't work in fiction. I've only seen it done once, when Tom Robbins used it in *Half-Asleep in Frog Pajamas*, but he is a master storyteller, with a string of successful novels to prove it. He's allowed to experiment once in a while. The rest of us stick to more easily workable forms.

First Person: This allows you to write as if it were you telling your story. (I heard a scrabbling noise overhead. What should I do? I knew that Jake was out, so there was only me and whatever was in the attic.) It's a very powerful voice in that it permits real immediacy, but it's also very limited in that it makes it impossible for the writer to explore anything the narrator doesn't know about and participate in. You can't, for instance, show a clock counting down across town if the narration is in the first person. You can't show a scene in someone else's past. You can only show what the hero sees and experiences. I have, however, read at least one book (*Army of the Republic* by Stuart Archer Cohen) in which the author uses first person for each character. He does this by writing each chapter from the POV of a different character. This works, but it is a little confusing when you first start the chapter until you figure out who's mind you're in. If you should choose this POV, please title each chapter with the name of the character, so the reader knows who's speaking.

Another technique, which I've only seen used by Diana Gabaldon in her wonderful *Outlander* series, is to write the main character, Claire, in the First Person and then use the Third Person to show things the protagonist can't know, such as what's happening to Claire's husband, Jamie. It works very well in these books, though it does take a little getting used to. I'm tempted to try it myself in my next book.

Third Person, Omniscient (limited): This allows you to see the interiors of all your major characters and to be aware of events throughout the universe of your book. The limits are few, but there are some. First and foremost: avoid head jumping. This happens when you jump from one person's mind to another person's mind within one scene. It causes confusion. You can change viewpoints, but limit it to different scenes. You should also avoid getting into the heads of every single character in the book. Keep a limited omniscient point of view by only exploring the thoughts of those who really matter: the main characters. You can still visit places where events are unfolding in which none of your major characters has a part; these can be told in terms of what is seen and done from the view of an outsider or the narrator.

Tense: Do not write in the present tense unless you're writing a movie script or treatment. It rarely works in fiction. If you're not writing a movie script, stick to the past tense: She hurried toward the store and saw him hiding in the alley. What could she do? There was only the fact of the gun in her pocket and the horror in her mind. Without thinking, she pulled out the gun and took aim. And of course, don't mix tenses.

Exercises:

Write a simple scene in the third person omniscient point of view using the past tense.

Now rewrite the scene in the first person and in the past tense.

Go over what you've written and write down some of the ways in which each POV works.

WORKSHOP 10

THEME

Most themes are implied rather than stated, and are usually about society, human nature, or life in general. Themes explore ideas that are timeless and universal, yet not always clearly understood. Most stories project some kind of idea about life that can be understood as theme. For instance, in *The Scarlet Letter,* Nathanial Hawthorne establishes the theme on the first page by creating an image of a bleak stone jail entrance surrounded by beautiful climbing roses. This allows us to see immediately that the story is essentially about man and all his laws and rules against the thorny but beautiful realities of nature. Though Hawthorne never states that this is the theme of his work, the image says it for him.

In addition, he recalls this theme frequently throughout the story by exploring other images that juxtapose these two elements. *The Scarlet Letter* explores the classic theme of sin and redemption. The protagonist has committed some kind of crime or sin, and the action centers around his quest to atone for that deed. Throughout the story, he must struggle against his inner demons and desires in order to redeem himself. This theme is frequently used in modern literature and in movies.

Theme is usually subtle and not always easy to see; however, it's very important that you, as the writer, know what your central themes are. Theme may be strongly related to the dramatic moment, so you need to be very clear on this. If your theme is man against the machine, for example, and your dramatic moment is an image of a man being turned into a cyborg, it's necessary to remember this as you write.

This is may turn out to be even more important after the book is written and you're getting comments from your friends and other critics. Clearly understanding your theme and dramatic moment will enable you to listen to criticism and use the constructive parts without losing track of what's essential to your story.

Exercise:

Think about the underlying theme(s) that support the conflict in your book, and then think of objects that can personify that theme. Like Hawthorne's roses on a jailhouse wall, can you come up with something concrete that can be used to show the theme without you ever stating it?

WORKSHOP 11

ARENA OR SETTING

Your story exists in a time and place, and you must know that world intimately so that you can recreate it in the mind of the reader. Where does the action take place? Is it in the present? In the past? In a galaxy far, far away? In more than one time? Or is it in some fantastical place of your own design? Remember, your characters don't exist in a vacuum, and the world around them will affect their lives in myriad ways.

Where the action takes place will affect many details of the story. For example, if your book is written in the past, people will dress differently and speak differently than they do today. How will you handle their speech? Will your dialogue mimic the dialect of the time, or will you use bits of dialect to give the flavor of the time without making it too difficult to read? If the story takes place on a ship, you will use different metaphors than you would if you were describing the same action during a war. You might say "he was drowning in an ocean of sweat" on the ship, while in a battle, he'd probably be "sweating bullets." (Well, not really because that's a cliché, but you get the idea.)

If there's a war going on, even if your characters don't actively participate in it, and your action takes place outside it, your story will be affected by its existence. The fact of the war becomes part of the arena or setting, not part of the plot. For example, in *The Diary of Anne*

Frank, the story takes place in an attic, in a house, in Germany, in the midst of a war. The characters do not go out shooting and killing people; they are not soldiers. All the action is personal and takes place in the attic, but the arena shapes that space.

Exercises:

Write down the answers in your notebook:

1. When does your novel take place? Past, present, future, fantasy time, end of time, beginning of time, outside of time? Describe in detail.

2. Where does your story take place? What city, what nation, what world?

3. Who runs this world? Are your characters among the elite or are they just ordinary people?

4. How do the politics of the time and place affect your characters? Do they rebel? Are they supporters of the status quo?

5. What is going on in the world around your characters? What is the socio/political climate?

WORKSHOP 12

WHAT IS YOUR MAIN CONFLICT?

Although there may be more than one conflict in the story, there has to be at least one central conflict between the protagonist and the antagonist. This is where "us" and "them" come in. This is where you, the author, define good and evil. Without conflict, stories become boring. If you've been doing the work so far, you should understand your idea, your dramatic moment, and have some sense of your characters. Now you can use that knowledge to discover how conflict works to further develop these emerging parts.

The conflict should, in the deepest sense, begin to tell us who your hero and his enemy really are. Let's say we have a bird on the branch of a tree, and a cat comes into the paragraph and begins stalking the bird. That's a conflict. That's Tweety and Sylvester. Between the antagonist and the hero, there can be no peace: cops and robbers, cops and drug lords, lawyers and polluters, man against the hurricane, man against the sea, the volcano, the asteroid, environmental disaster, disease, social convention, and on and on. Your conflict can involve a clash of cultures (Turk and Greek, Jew and Arab, man and woman), or you can have a man and a woman fall in love despite the clash of their cultures: *Romeo and Juliet, West Side Story*. Before anything can happen to change the characters or bring the plot into existence, we must establish a conflict.

Frequently, the conflict centers around an object that both the protagonist and the antagonist pursue. It could be a person (a love interest), or it might be a thing—a magic sword, a computer chip, a lost treasure, a hidden secret—that is sought by both parties and around which the plot is set in motion. In the movie, *National Treasure*, the object of the conflict is the treasure. In *The Fifth Element*, the object of the conflict is the earth itself. Will evil destroy it before Leelu can save it?

Sometimes, the object of the conflict is not so clear. In *Hamlet*, for example, the antagonist is death itself, and its agent is Hamlet's uncle, the man who killed the king in order to be with the queen, Hamlet's mother, and to take over the kingdom. The ostensible object of his pursuit is the woman and the kingdom, and Hamlet's purpose in exposing him is to obtain justice, and save the mother and the kingdom. But the real antagonist in this story is death; thus both Hamlet and the uncle die in the end, as does the queen, and the uncle's agent, the killer of Hamlet. When death is the antagonist, no one wins.

Exercises:
Describe the two different points of view that must clash and create your conflict.

What is the conflict really about? Is it about death? About revenge? About fear?

What are the underlying theme(s) that support the conflict?

Who is "us," and who is "them?"

Is there an object of the conflict, and if so, what is it?

WORKSHOP 13

WHAT IS THE RESOLUTION TO THE MAIN CONFLICT?

You must know your ending before you begin to write your story. Otherwise, you run the risk of going off on a tangent and getting lost. Your beginning and end are signposts that keep you on the road, so figure out your ending now. In the end, the conflict must be resolved; the hero must save the world; the bad guys must be destroyed—or at least put out of commission until the sequel. You could also end in tragedy. The hero loses; the world is not saved, but this may be less satisfying to the reader. You're the writer, so it's up to you. Personally, I prefer my fiction to end happily, but there are many readers who like a good nightmare.

The main conflict takes place between the hero and his enemy and will have an outcome. They will fight (literally or metaphorically), and either the hero will win or he will lose. The girl will be won, or she will be sacrificed; the disease will be conquered, or the survivors will run for their lives; the invaders will be repelled, or they will take over the city. To make it simple: How does it all turn out? Remember, most readers prefer that there be a clear, unequivocal ending in which the hero either wins or dies. Ambiguity in the ending is frustrating. However....

Is your ending the true ending, or are you planning a sequel? If you are planning a sequel, have you truly ended the action of this particular part of the story? An ending that's merely a cliffhanger, which leaves many loose ends, is not satisfying to the reader, so be careful. Make sure you tie it all up and still leave the reader with a thirst for more.

Exercises:

Think about these questions and make notes:

Is your ending happy or tragic?

Is the antagonist defeated or does he live on to fight another day?

Will you prepare the reader for the ending? If so, how?

Is there a turning point (a decision or event) that sends the hero down the path toward either destruction or redemption?

WORKSHOP 14

WHAT OTHER CONFLICTS ARISE?

From the moment he or she opens the book until the climax and resolution, there will be moments of drama and conflict that keep the reader continually on edge. In fact, every scene should center on a conflict of some kind. No one wants to read about how the heroine fixed dinner and put the kids to bed. Unless there's some conflict there, either implied or happening during the scene (he still wasn't home, she watched the clock, dinner burned, the children screamed, there was a noise in the basement), there will be no interest. Conflict keeps our minds on the book. Without conflict, we might as well be reading a shopping list.

Name some of the conflicts that will take place in some of the scenes you're going to write:

How do these conflicts help advance the main conflict? For instance, if the main conflict is about marital infidelity, do other conflicts deal with related themes? Lack of trust, lack of support, selfishness?

Are your conflicts concrete? Do you use real objects, people, animals, and things to dramatize your scenes? For example, when you show two lovers breaking up, do you break *things* in order to make it concrete? Say, in the last part of the scene, the man grabs the woman's wrist and the beaded bracelet he gave her comes apart. Can't you hear the beads rattling onto the tile floor, each one echoing inside the hollow of her heart? Describe such a scene in detail.

TELLING THE STORY

WORKSHOP 15

SHOW. DON'T TELL

So how do you show people who your characters are? In a book, you can tell us what they think, how they react inwardly to the circumstances of their lives, and we can listen in on how they've been hurt, what secret grudges they harbor. But is that the best way to show character? If we were talking about a movie, rather than a book, we would say that the *only* way to show character is through action. It's what a character *does* that shows us who he is. However, we're not writing a movie; we're writing a book, and that gives us more options.

It's vital to learn to show, rather than tell. It's usually the most effective way to get your story across. Showing is not just a way to expand on character; it's also the best way to present the details of your plot. By showing us character in action, you can also advance the plot, introduce or solve a problem, or set up a later scene most effectively. It also lessens the risk of boring your reader.

We show character in action by creating scenes in which events happen. Every scene should be important to the story. It should tell us something about the character, advance the plot, or introduce important background information. Here's an example of a scene:

> Stumbling through the dark, Judy closed the bathroom door and turned on the light, confirming the warm wetness between her legs in bright blooms of red. Crying out, she fell, bruising her knees on the cold marble. But physical pain could not penetrate her panicked race down the frozen trails of her heart.
> "Judy!" David knocked on the bathroom door, as if they hadn't been married for more than five years. "What's wrong?"
> He knew what was wrong. How could he not know? Why did she have to say it? Flinging open the door, she stood in the glaring light and let his eyes feast on the screaming red stains on her pajama bottoms. His face reflected her misery, and as the anger subsided, she knew words were no longer necessary. "I lost the baby," she said anyway.
> David wrapped his arms around her and pulled her close. "Oh, baby," he whispered, and despite herself, Judy wept.

And here's an example of the same scene being told to the reader instead of being shown:

> Judy stood in the cold bathroom, contemplating the color red. There was no way she could avoid the conclusion closing in on her, and a cry escaped her lips as she fell to the floor. How had this happened again? she wondered. Why did it keep happening to her? What would

she tell David? Sorry, hon, I seem to have lost the baby again?

Can you see how much more immediate and compelling the scene is in the first example?

Exercises:

What are some of the character traits you want to show in your hero?

Describe a scene that shows us these traits. How does he or she act? What does he or she do?

If your hero is changed by the action of the story, describe exactly what changes.

WORKSHOP 16

THE PLOT

The plot of the story is the series of events that take place. Plot is what happens. It includes decisions and actions made by the characters, as well as results of those decisions and actions. Plot includes outside events that influence the outcome and obstacles thrown in the path of the protagonist. Simply, plot is a summary of the action. Plot is what happens.

The plot has a structure. In the beginning of the story, the characters and conflict are introduced. Then there's a turning point where the protagonist commits to the action. The next part of the plot is what happens as the protagonist and antagonist vie for supremacy. There is a climax and finally a denouement. We've already discussed this as a sexual metaphor.

Note that there is a difference between plot and story. Plot is what happens, but story is the way that plot is revealed to the reader. Techniques like flashback, holding back information, and sometimes, even revealing events out of order, are all ways to tell the story. Straight chronology is not necessarily the best method.

Exercises:

Briefly describe the plot of your story and ask yourself these questions:

1. Is your plot predictable? Will readers know what's going to happen before it happens?

2. Is your ending a surprise, or is it expected? If your ending is obvious, you'll need to come up with something that is not.

3. Has it been done before? (Of course, it has. According to experts, there are only thirty-six actual dramatic plots.) What then, is different about yours? What can you do to make it original?

4. Does your plot have momentum? Does it build to a climax?

WORKSHOP 17

SUBGOALS AND PLOT TWISTS

The hero and antagonist are each working toward their own goals. They both want the plot inspired by their conflict to be resolved in a way that satisfies their mutually exclusive intentions. The hero wants to save the world. The antagonist wants to destroy it. The hero wants to save his love from the antagonist, who wants to keep her for himself, no matter what the cost. The hero wants to find the treasure and so does the antagonist, but one will do it for the good of all and the other for his own selfish ends. The hero wants to defeat death and save the city from the plague. The plague wants to kill everyone.

This main goal will be achieved or not in the end, but along the way, the hero and other characters will have subgoals that must be attained first. For instance, in *Back to the Future*, before Michael J. Fox's character can get back to the future and save Doc (his main goal), he has to: 1) find a way to get fuel for the DeLorean, 2) get his parents to meet and fall in love, 3) get them to kiss at the dance, and so forth. Each subgoal may lead to another, and it is the *failure* of the hero to attain the subgoal that advances the plot, keeps it unpredictable, and keeps it moving.

These moments are called plot twists or reversals. Here is where you plan for failure and set up the plot twists that keep readers turning pages.

Exercises:

Take some time to think about and write the answers to these questions:

1.   What is the hero's first subgoal?

2.   How does the hero plan to attain this subgoal?

3.   What does the reader expect to happen when the hero attempts to achieve the subgoal?

4.   How did you set up these expectations in the reader?

5.   Does the antagonist or the course of events foil this subgoal? If so, how?

6.   What is the hero's second subgoal?

7.   How does the hero plan to attain this subgoal?

8.   What does the reader expect to happen when the hero attempts to achieve the subgoal?

9.   How did you set up these expectations in the reader?

10. Does the antagonist or the course of events foil this subgoal? If so, how?

11. What is the hero's third subgoal? How do you set it up?

12. How does the hero plan to attain this subgoal?

13. What does the reader expect to happen when the hero attempts to achieve the subgoal?

14. How did you set up these expectations in the reader?

15. Does the antagonist or the course of events foil this subgoal? If so, how?

No matter how many subgoals you have, you should use these questions to help you clarify the action and how it will all play out.

WORKSHOP 18

PIVOTAL PLOT POINTS

In every story, there are critical turning points, scenes in which decisions are made, or in which complications or reversals take place. These events change the direction of the action and propel the characters forward. Whenever the story changes direction because of problems or conflicts, it is a pivotal scene. Think of it in terms of the roller coaster. If the story is the car, then whenever the car changes direction—going up, down, or swinging around—that moment of change is a pivotal plot point. There are several in every story. Here are the most important ones:

- The opening scene or inciting event
    - This is the opening of the book. This scene gets the reader involved and sets up the conflict and the story.

- The point-of-no-return scene (the kiss)
    - This scene occurs early in the story when the hero commits to his role in resolving the conflict and can no longer turn back. In *Back to the Future*, this is when Marty gets in the DeLorean to flee the terrorists who shot Doc. Accelerating to 88 mph, he is zapped into the past.

- Major complications and plot twists (there may be several of these)
    - These are reversals and plot twists that prevent the hero from confronting the antagonist and saving the day.

- The climax
    - At last, the hero and antagonist meet face-to-face and have it out. I*n Back to the Future*, this is when Marty finally (in the past) gets the DeLorean in motion, speeding up to 88 mph just as lightning strikes the clock tower.

In addition, there are scenes between these scenes that are also pivotal. For instance, in the beginning, you start with a dramatic event, your opening scene. From there the action turns, and you might give a little background on your main character's situation. This setup begins to get more tense and then suddenly, a decision must be made. This brings us to the point-of-no-return scene, in which the hero commits to the action of the plot.

If we could draw this graphically, it would look something like this:

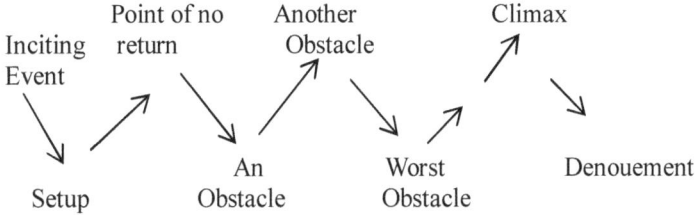

Each of the arrows shows the direction of the action in

terms of the reader's response. If the reader is experiencing a rising feeling of terror or suspense, then the arrow will point up. If the reader is feeling less excited and heading toward merely being interested, then the arrow will point down. This is called rising action or falling action. It's your job to make sure the action never falls so low that the reader gets tired and bored, and to make sure that the action sometimes excites the reader so much that he cannot put the book down.

Remember, variety really is the spice of life. No one wants to be kept on edge for so long that it's unbearable, any more than they want to be mildly interested for long periods. It's the changing emotions, the storm of emotions created by the writer, that keeps readers turning pages.

WORKSHOP 19

DEFINING YOUR PIVOTAL PLOT POINTS

Here is where you can start to lay out the major struts of your plot. You may want to take notes first, then when you're sure, you can write each plot point on index cards to begin setting up the structure of your novel. You can also use the forms that have been provided in the back of this book.

Think about what happens in the opening scene. How are you going to set up your conflict and show us who your characters are? You can use more than one scene, but the one that turns the direction of the reader's emotions and begins to increase the tension or momentum is the pivotal scene. In your notebook, sketch each of these pivotal scenes out now.

1. What is your inciting event, your opening scene?
    A. Which characters are involved?
    B. What happens?
    C. What is the main conflict?
    D. What's the purpose of the scene?
    E. What objects, smells, tastes, textures, and sounds do you want to use?
    F. What's the emotional distance?
    G. Will there be a cliffhanger?

2. Now ask the same questions of these other pivotal scenes:

    A. Point-of-no-return scene

    B. First obstacle or reversal

    C. Second obstacle or reversal

    D. Worst obstacle or reversal so far

    E. Climactic scene. Explain in detail.

WORKSHOP 20

SUBPLOTS

Since all the characters in your novel have their own reality, their own motivations and conflicts, subplots will exist. Whether they're important enough for you to pay them heed, has to do with whether they relate to the main plot. For instance, in *Overboard*, the character of Andrew, Joanna Staton's butler on board the yacht acts as a kind of mirror to Joanna in that it is her treatment of him in the beginning, and his mimicry of her near the end, that shows us just how small she was and how far she's come. We don't know much about him, but that he quits his job in the end confirms our belief that he's a real person, not just a mirror, and that he, too, has been affected by the drama. His story, minor though it is, supports the main story. He, too, is seeking a deeper reality than is found aboard the yacht. Joanna's courage in jumping overboard to join her love, gives him the courage to quit his job (his own way of jumping overboard) and move forward with his life.

Subplots are often generated by minor characters and deal with similar conflicts to those found in the main plot. A subplot looks at the same issues as the main plot, but from the point of view of a relatively minor character. Though the values and beliefs of the minor character can be completely different from that of the hero or the antagonist, the resolution of the subplot will in some way strengthen or give emphasis to the main themes of the story. (If you don't know anything about this yet, don't worry. You can come back to this later.)

Subplots are important, however, because they add depth to the characters and make them seem more real and substantial.

Sometimes a subplot can be pivotal to the story, becoming a set of obstacles that have to be overcome, so that the hero can move on to resolving the main conflict. For instance, in *Back to the Future*, the main conflict has to do with Marty getting the DeLorean working so he can go back, but a subplot develops in which his father and mother almost don't fall in love because of him. This sets up a whole new set of obstacles that must be overcome before he can attend to his main problem.

Exercises:

1.　Are any of your minor characters involved in a subplot?

2.　How does this subplot relate to your main plot?

3.　In what ways will you show this relationship?

4.　Where will these two separate plots intersect?

WORKSHOP 21

THE PLOT REVISITED

Go over your plot outline again and fill it out or change it as needed, taking into consideration your characters in relation to the plot, subgoals, subplots, and pivotal plot points. If you've created pivotal scene cards, put them in the proper order. These now form a skeleton, which you begin to knit together using additional scenes. Each pivotal scene is a signpost. Ask yourself, "What comes next?" Then start filling in the spaces between these pivotal scenes with other scenes. If you keep the next pivotal scene in front of you, you'll be able to stay on track.

When you're finished, you should be able to lay out all your scene cards on the floor or tape them up on your wall and see the entire plot of the novel spread out before you. This will be of inestimable help when it comes time to actually write the book.

Do I actually do it this way? Usually no. I write a treatment, showing all the main scenes, so that it will keep me from going off on a tangent, but I've read some novels that are so complex with so many different plots and subplots going on, it seems likely that it must be done like this, and I have a plan for a series of books that will have to be set up in this way.

WORKSHOP 22

THE BEGINNING OF YOUR STORY

Use your notebook to begin laying out your story. Break down the beginning of your story into its own beginning, middle, and end. Remember that the beginning will introduce the characters, establish motivations, and initiate the plot. The beginning of your story will end in the "kiss." This is the point, metaphorically, at which the character will commit to the act itself. Think about breaking this down in terms of falling in love and engaging in sex. If this makes you uncomfortable, think about it in terms of a roller coaster. Either way, the middle of the beginning will show us who the main characters are. Just remember to show us characters in action. Don't tell us about them.

The beginning of the beginning: This is where the two (reader and writer) are attracted. The writer gets the reader's attention and shows that he can be trusted to tell a good story. The characters may be introduced in an attention-getting scene.

The middle of the beginning: Here the characters are introduced. The reader should be enchanted, amused, interested, and above all, curious.

The end of the beginning. This scene commits both the writer and the reader to the act. The reader should be ready to participate fully, to identify with the protagonist. This scene ends in the kiss. In *Harry Potter*, this would be the moment when Hagrid says, "Ye're a wizard, Harry!" In *Back to the Future*, it would be when the DeLorean hits 88mph and Marty is zapped into the past. In *The Scarlet Letter*, it would be the moment when Hester Prine exits the jail with that beautifully embroidered "A" on her dress. In *Dead Until Dark*, it would be when Sookie saves Bill, the vampire, from the drainers. In *The Fifth Element*, it's the moment that Corbin Dallas decides not to hand the beautiful Leelu over to the police. Think of some of the movies you've seen and books you've read and identify this moment in them.

Finally, ask yourself these questions about your story. Some of these may be difficult to answer.

1. In the beginning of your story, what emotions will you draw from the reader?

2. Is your reader ready to move on?

3. Is he committed to getting involved with you?

4. Will he agree to identify with your character and move on to the next phase of your relationship?

5. Have you achieved empathy?

WORKSHOP 23

THE MIDDLE OF YOUR STORY

For the writer and reader, the middle of the story is the act itself. Now you will show the action, the push and pull, give and take of relationship, the relationships between the characters and the relationship between you, the writer, and your reader. In this part of the story, you will cause the reader to feel a range of emotions you've designed for him by throwing obstacles in front of the hero and then showing how the hero overcomes these obstacles. The middle begins when the characters commit to the action, and the middle ends when the climactic scene begins. This is where your subgoals and plot twists will be most useful. Just remember to show your characters in action.

The beginning of the middle. The hero becomes aware of the situation, and begins looking for a solution. Your first obstacle is set up, and you'll create the first reversal that will prevent the protagonist solving the main conflict. Ideally, this reversal should lead into the next obstacle.

> In *Back to the Future*, Marty realizes he's in the past and goes looking for the Doc of that time, but when Doc looks at the DeLorean, he realizes that without plutonium, there's no way to fuel the journey. They soon realize they can solve this by timing the trip

to the lightning that struck the clock tower.

The middle of the middle. The second major obstacle will be more dramatic than the first, more intense, and will lead into the next problem.

> So Marty's exploring the '50s and is in the malt shop when his father comes in and gets into it with George McFly, Marty's father. A new subplot develops in the form of Biff, and then Lorraine, as Marty gets embroiled in his parent's lives and sets the next big set of obstacles in motion: his mother falls in love with him instead of his father, so if he doesn't fix things, he will disappear from the future altogether.

The end of the middle. This final complication sets up the rising action that will bring about the climax. At this point, nothing is settled. There is no easy resolution to this problem.

> Example: Marty and Doc have a plan but time is running out. Marty has to make sure his mother falls in love with his father, but he ends up locked in a trunk. The clock is ticking, and more importantly, the audience is on the edge of their seats.

Step back and think about the middle of your story. What emotions will your scenes draw from the reader? Can you intensify them? Can you make the reader go crazy with desire to reach a conclusion?

WORKSHOP 24
THE END OF YOUR STORY

Now let's repeat the process for the end of the story. Break down the end of your tale into its own beginning, middle, and end. Remember that the end will begin with the climactic scene. The hero will win or lose. The world will be saved. The girl will be rescued. This is the point, metaphorically, at which the characters expose themselves completely. Doubt is cast off. All pretense is exposed. After the climax, everything is resolved, justice is done, and loose ends are tied up. Just remember characters in action. Show. Don't tell.

The beginning of the end. This is the climactic scene. The hero wins or loses. Everything that has gone before has brought you to this place. In reality, this moment is how babies are made. In art, this is where the artist pulls everything together and makes it all work. It's where writer and reader join in complete understanding and rapport.

> To continue our example of *Back to the Future*, here is where Marty gets out of the trunk and ends up on stage, but he's slowly disappearing as it becomes less and less likely that George and Lorraine will ever kiss. Hope is almost lost, and then George

suddenly stands up like a man and takes the girl. Marty recovers and the second obstacle is resolved.

The middle of the end. There's still the major obstacle to overcome. Now is the final bout between the real antagonist and the hero.

> In *Back to the Future*, the enemy is not Biff or any of the problems Marty's had to overcome, the real antagonist is being lost in time, and now is the showdown. Marty still has to get back to the DeLorean and be on time for the lightning. Doc, in the meantime, is having his own troubles getting the mechanics set up, and then the car won't start. Finally, the car takes off; the lightning strikes and Marty is back.

The end of the end. This is where all loose ends are tied off. The hero is safe. The world is as it should be. Of course, sometimes it's a little better than it was.

> In Marty's case, his interaction with his father in the past has been enough to push his father into the career he's always wanted. And in this new future, Marty has a cool car and Jennifer is waiting, but lest we get too complacent, here comes Doc with a new DeLorean and an invitation to the next adventure.

Now review your ending and analyze the beginning, middle and end. What emotions did you draw from the reader? Is your reader happy or sad now that it's over?

Would he want to engage in a second emotional experience with you? If the answer is no, then you need to go back over these pages and rethink some of it.

WORKSHOP 25

FLASHBACKS

Sometimes it works to tell your story chronologically, starting at the beginning and moving toward the end, but sometimes it doesn't. In that case, the answer is the flashback. A flashback can be short, encompassing a few scenes or a WORKSHOP, or it can take up the entire book. For instance, in *Memoirs of a Geisha*, the story begins in the present, giving us little more than the sense that we are looking backward through the eyes of the geisha. On the second page, it flashes back to her childhood, and the story begins.

Flashbacks are used for many reasons. In movies, they're often used to get the star on the screen from the first, rather than waiting until the childhood scene is played out, but they also serve dramatic purposes. The flashback allows us to provide information about the past when it's needed and not before. It also allows us to get the reader interested in a part of the storyline that may be really exciting before moving into the aftermath. For example, when a flashback is used to show a murder in the midst of the investigation. This provides excitement. A flashback can also be used to hide information. Instead of revealing what's going on now, the writer flashes back to the past.

There's a lot that can be done with the flashback, which is why it's so widely used.

Exercises:
1. Will you use flashbacks in your book?
2. How will you use them?
3. What will they accomplish?

WHO IS IT ALL ABOUT?

WORKSHOP 26

GOOD AND EVIL

God and the Devil. Dorothy and the Wicked Witch. Harry Potter and Voldemort. I'm sure you can think of a hundred other hero-villain pairs, but what is good and evil? Can one exist without the other? Can we show what is good without evil to darken its edges? Or penetrate the murk of evil without light? Is the existence of evil necessary to the definition of good? Can any story exist without conflict? Although these questions may be generally unanswerable, it's important for the writer to understand that fiction is an attempt to find answers anyway.

Let's attempt to define these two concepts in terms of character. Evil characters are often liars, without empathy or compassion. We see them behaving with cruelty toward others. Evil characters usually use their power to corrupt others, to lead them to destruction and death, and inspire fear in others. Good people, on the other hand, are compassionate, empathic, and altruistic. They reveal themselves in acts of kindness and use their personal power for the benefit of all, inspiring love in others. On one hand, we have deception, selfishness, cruelty, hatred, and fear, and on the other, we have kindness, generosity, love, courage, and honesty.

But good people can lie, so it's not lies that define evil; it's the intent behind those lies. If the intent is to protect or help others, then the liar is good. Think of *Jakob, the Liar* starring Robin Williams. In this story, Jakob lies to his son so the child won't realize they're living in a concentration camp. We could hardly call this deception evil.

Can we watch someone hurting and feel nothing? Doctors and dentists do it all the time. If they felt the pain of their patients, they'd never be able to treat them. So we forgive them their lack of empathy. If a doctor tries to save someone and causes that person pain in the process, we call that good because the intent is good. Depending on the intent, it is sometimes kind to be cruel.

Is it evil to take and good to be generous? People can give with evil intent. A person could give someone else a house and a beautiful life, but do it for control or power, to use that person for selfish reasons. Think of Julia Roberts in *Sleeping with the Enemy*. Although the husband gave her everything, he did it with evil intent. She escaped by faking her own death, causing him misery and grief, yet this selfishness on her part is seen as self-defense, and she is seen as good. He gives her everything and is evil, and she takes everything from him (even his life) and is good. So we can see that good is not necessarily giving, and evil is not necessarily taking. Many of what we call evil acts are actually not evil in themselves. The intent behind the act defines it.

Often, good and evil comes down to a story of us and them. In any conflict between us and them, *they* are always going to be defined as evil, and *we* are going to be defined as good. In the end, good and evil are frequently a matter of which side you're on, because in reality, there is no such thing as absolute evil. Good people kill, and so do evil ones. In real life, these concepts are so tangled, it's sometimes impossible to tell them apart.

However, the purpose of fiction is to try to do just that. Take the old story about cowboys and Indians. Each side has its rationale, its share of evil deeds, and its motivations, and in the end, it's the angle from which the author tells the story that determines who is good and who is evil. *The Last of the Mohicans* as it was originally written by James Fenimore Cooper portrays one point of view, *Dances with Wolves*, another. Along the way, the author selects facts according to his own beliefs and knowledge, and perhaps without even meaning to, distorts the evidence.

We think we know the difference between good and evil. We point to historical examples: Nazis could not be called the good guys (except perhaps to other Nazis), and it would be difficult, if not impossible, to think of Gandhi as evil. Yet someone shot Gandhi, so someone thought he was evil. Sages have been burned for heresy throughout history, and genocide is always justified by those who inflict it.

As the author, you must choose your side, and define "us" and "them." What matters to a writer is how to make someone, some character, *appear* good or evil. This is done by showing the intent behind the behavior and can be handled through dialogue, exposition (talking about it), and always through action.

Remember, the distance between art and reality is very fine, and whole cultures can be shaped by the thoughts of people who write things down. The pen really is "mightier than the sword." Hence, ideas of absolute good and evil pervade our culture. As writers, we can perpetuate the dualistic thinking that makes it possible for people to be manipulated by ideas of "us" and "them," or we can show that our adversaries are human, too, despite our own desire to find only evil in those we fear.

*FATAL FLAWS AND SAVING GRACES

No one can be perfectly good, nor can anyone be perfectly evil, so every hero is flawed in some way, and every antagonist must have some saving grace. A hero's fatal flaw is a character flaw that can figure into the story in a big way. Think of Marty in *Back to the Future*. He could never back down from a dare. This trait almost gets him killed more than once, and it creates the sequel to the first film because his refusal to back down in a car race causes the accident that ruins his life in the future. In another story, Orson Scott Card's *Ender's Game*, Ender's fatal flaw is an inability to back down in a fight. He's a small boy, so he fights to the death rather than having to fight again. He hates this in himself, yet this trait leads him to win the war and save the earth. This trait also propels him into the second book, forcing him to leave earth.

On the other side of the coin, the antagonist cannot be perfectly evil. He must have a saving grace: some little thing about him that is good. Imagine a Nazi concentration camp murderer, the absolute personification of evil. His saving grace is that he truly loves his wife. When the Allies arrive, this goodness in him leads to his death because he turns back to save her.

WORKSHOP 27

IDENTIFICATION AND PERSON – IFICATION

Many years ago, I was writing my thesis for an MA in Communication. I had read at least a hundred books and articles, and my mind was being torn apart by the many conflicting ideas I had to reconcile.

Then one night, I had a dream. In the dream, I was the watcher, and this is what I saw: First, there was a scene. It was a meadow. Not a real meadow, more like a cartoon, with green trees and yellow-green swaths of grass and an impossibly blue sky. Moving across the meadow was a little black man. Not like a real man at all. Not any shade of brown. More like the color of the night sky without the stars. Black. With stumpy little arms and legs and a head. Other than that, it had no features.

Then click. There was another scene. This time, it was a wide-open space with distant hills at sunset. Colors all orange and yellow with the dark silhouette of a palm tree in the foreground. There, once again, was the little black creature, walking across the landscape. Click: another scene. This time, I was observing a seascape, with the ocean meeting the shore. The sky was blue and so was the sea. The little black man bounced along the shore. Then another cartoon landscape and then another, each featuring the same little creature.

When I woke, I realized that the dream had made sense

of the issues with which I was battling. How could so many intelligent people examine the same concept—communication—and come to such completely different conclusions? Here in the dream was my answer.

The little black critter was the idea: communication. Each landscape he walked through was the mind of one of the theorists whose work I had been reading. Each scholar looked at the idea through the paradigm, the lens, of his own experience and knowledge. Thus each one studied the same thing, but saw it in a different way. Most of the time, they were describing the setting—the state of their own minds—rather than the idea itself.

The result was confusion and competition, and the funny thing is that these people had made communication the object of their study. They weren't communicating, not really. Oh yes, they were getting their positions across, describing their knowledge, but each was competing with the others for supremacy by insisting that the landscape of their own ideas was the reality.

This made my thesis a little easier. I was able to use the ideas presented by each scholar and not have to pick the right one, because each one was true *from the perspective* of the thinker. What I could do was filter these ideas through my own landscape, my own experience, and choose the parts of each that made sense to me and fitted into my own theories. Dah dah! Finished the thesis; got the degree.

Truth is, though, more important than the degree (to me anyway), was the dream, and now, years later, I still think about it. I'm still learning from it. Some scholars understand this failing in human communication, and even try to explain it to college students, but no one gets it until they get it. However, because some theorists understand how much the paradigm is a part of the communication—the medium is the message—there are rules when writing papers for scholarly review that include defining terms.

Realizing that many of the terms we use to communicate are highly abstract and often reflect the mind of the thinker more than they do the idea under discussion, scholarly papers almost always begin with definitions of the terms to be used. For instance, words like freedom, justice, work, abuse can mean many, many different things to different people. Freedom might mean living outside the walls of prison for a convict, but to a person who lives in society, it might mean escaping on a boat and living at sea.

This slipperiness of abstract ideas is part of what makes it so difficult to communicate, and is the reason that semantics is so often the problem. Much of our time trying to communicate is spent on aligning paradigms and checking to make sure we're all on the same page, rather than actually reaching out to each other mind to mind.

In stories, we use several techniques to overcome such barriers to communication. In a story about freedom, we wouldn't explain that we mean this rather than that. Instead, we might create a character who personifies our abstraction. Perhaps we'd have a character who lives on a boat like John D. McDonald's Travis McGee, or two characters running from the dogs chasing them, chained together at the ankle. These stories both talk about freedom, but they never mention the word. They describe freedom by making it real, by giving it depth and dimension and personality. By personifying[1] the abstract, they make it concrete.

This is a start, but there's so much more. Stories are the only way we ever really touch each other mind to mind. A well-executed story by a master storyteller is an experience that can change us and open our minds to another reality. Through stories, we learn, not just intellectually, but viscerally, about different ways of looking at the world, and the more stories we read, the more we know about the human experience. Stories put us inside the world of the author's mind not as observers, but as participants.

Understanding this, it's easy to see why television, movies, the internet, and video games have so much power. Why they have so much hold on the minds of our children. Unlike books, which provide the experience without the visuals, these games manipulate every aspect of what's going on, leaving nothing to the imagination of the viewer. It's the most direct way we have of touching other minds, but in the wrong hands (and there probably aren't many right hands), these powerful technologies have altered and informed the minds of millions, but that's a topic for another article.

While books do not have the same power as movies or video games, they can provide a deeper experience, more meaning, and longer exposure. Because they are not as manipulative as other means of communication, books are not usually objectionable. Books leave the

---

[1] Personification usually refers to animals being portrayed as human, but for the purposes of this book, it will mean this process of making abstract ideas concrete, turning ideas into characters.

reader with choices, and allow him to participate on his own terms.

Regardless of the medium, the purpose of storytelling is to communicate. However, unlike scholars, who define words and try to explain their ideas, often in ways that are only of interest to other scholars, storytellers have to use other methods to get their ideas across. The purpose of the story as opposed to non-fiction is to create an experience in the mind of the participant, and that means the writer has to get the reader involved. This is often done by bypassing the intellect (at least at first) and appealing to the emotions.

We have all experienced the feeling of being hooked by a story, but how does it happen? How is it possible to get a reader to leave his own intellectual landscape behind and enter the one that the writer has created for him? We can see how it's done by reading the works of the best. One technique is identification. Storytellers cannot hook us on a story without getting us to identify with the protagonist.

Two stories that do this in a way that's both expert and obvious (if you're looking) come to mind: *Ender's Game* by Orson Scott Card and *Harry Potter* by J.K. Rowling. In the first book, Ender is a small boy with a dangerous, and maybe psychotic, older brother who just might kill him. Since he lives in a world where couples are only allowed two children, and he's a *third,* he's constantly teased (often violently) by the other kids in school.

We identify with Ender, but we're also afraid for him. Poor little Ender. We know how he feels. Luckily, he's constantly watched by the same people who allowed his birth, so the rage of others is contained. Then one day, the monitor is removed, and Ender is on his own against the kids in school and against his brother. I won't give the story away, but suffice it to say that Ender triumphs and our identification is complete. We are hooked.

Harry Potter's plight is similar. Harry's aunt and uncle make him live under the stairs in what amounts to a closet. If that's not bad enough, they abuse him emotionally day in and day out, showing extreme preference to their own nasty offspring. Poor Harry. We feel for him, and we know how he feels because we've all had moments when we felt that the entire world was against us, that it was all so unfair. When Harry learns that he's a wizard, that's even better because we all have daydreamed at some time or other in our lives, perhaps when we felt most unappreciated, that we were somehow special and unique and different from all the rest. Yes, in this way, we *are* Harry. Thus we are carried forward into the story and completely hooked.

This process of identification is the method authors use to entice us to enter the world of the story. By appealing to emotions shared by many people, writers turn readers into the protagonist, thus completing the process of identification. With stories featuring children, it's easy to see these emotional buttons, because we all recognize the common denominators of experience for children.

Few of us have gotten through our childhood without feeling small, abused, unappreciated, powerless, and afraid. We all have wished to be bigger, stronger, more powerful and better able to fend for ourselves. With adult stories, the process may be more subtle, but it is the same process. Find the common denominators for your audience and learn to push these emotional buttons.

Sympathy and Empathy

As in life, there are two ways of comprehending the reality of others: through sympathy or empathy. These are actually so close in meaning that we often confuse them. However, sympathy means to feel together, to suffer with, but empathy means to feel into, to enfold one inside the feelings of the other. Therefore, sympathy implies duality; there must be at least two people in order for sympathy to exist. Empathy, on the other hand, takes the feelings of one *into* the other and makes them one, thus empathy implies unity, or better yet, identity.

This is an important point, because, as the writer, your job is to get the reader to identify with your character. You do this by creating empathy for the character. First, the reader feels sympathetic toward this other person, but a skilled author will get him to go even further, to cross the line between self and other. Think of *The Kite Runner* by Khaled Hosseini. At first, the characters are so different from us. Part of a strange culture, they live in a world we've never seen. Yet, as the story unfolds, we begin to feel universal feelings: love, fear, betrayal, loss. By the time the author reveals the terrible thing he did and the dreadful remorse that motivates him, we are already wholly submerged in his world. When we see what happens to his friend because of him, we cry.

Identification occurs when the reader of fiction becomes so involved in the character's story, that he or she *becomes* the protagonist [literally—from the

Greek—the first (proto) person in a conflict (agonist)]. This we know as empathy. As the reader loses himself in the character and the story, as the separation between reader and character becomes blurred, we have identity. One becomes the other.

Identification happens to the reader as he experiences the world of the book. Person-ification, on the other hand, is the process the *author* goes through in creating a person with whom the reader can identify. You probably know personification as the technique of giving human qualities to animals. You've seen it done a million times in Disney movies and in children's storybooks, but for our purposes, person-ification (with the hyphen) is what the author does to make a character into a person, so that the reader will feel empathy and become one with the character. Without this creation of a person out of nothing but words and ideas, the book cannot live.

There are techniques that the author can use to make this happen. For example, let's say we want to make an acquaintance into a friend. There are steps we take to accomplish this:

We have to stand out from the crowd, so we arouse their curiosity and interest. We can do this with humor, showing a sincere interest in *them*, by stating shared interests or goals, or any number of other strategies.

1) Once we get their attention, we make ourselves vulnerable by telling them about ourselves in an open and honest way. We don't blurt out everything we've ever done, good and bad, but we do let our true feelings show, including that desire to make friends. If they show the same inclination, we move onto the next steps.

2) As our friendship begins to grow, we exchange ideas, thoughts, jokes, and information. We do things together and begin to understand each other. We provoke their sympathy and understanding. They see how much we have in common, and they laugh with us or cry with us as the case may be. As we are also listening to them, we are experiencing the same sympathetic feelings for them.

3) Over time, this sympathy will sometimes grow into true empathy, at which point you and your friend become true friends or best friends. Making friends is a two-sided experience with a great deal of back and forth exchange. The author's job, however, is one-sided. The author has to get the reader to make friends with his character without the advantage of being able to listen as well as talk. Though the process is similar, the author has to do all the work alone, without any help from the friend he's trying to make.

There are probably as many ways to do this as there are stories. One author might show us a poor persecuted child like Harry Potter living under the stairs in his uncle's house and quickly gain our sympathy. While another might slowly draw us into the world of his story and bit-by-bit tear away the social masks to reveal the truth of his character (like Hosseini). Both methods work. Both show us the truth of the character, his vulnerable, undefended reality, and both rouse our sympathy, and then our empathy. When Hagrid says to Harry, "Ye're a wizard, Harry!" we're primed and ready to become him for the duration of the story.

Children's stories have this advantage: we've all been children, and we've all, at one time or another, felt that life was not fair. Thus it's easy to gain the reader's sympathy by showing the child hero being treated so badly, but it's when we see that the unfairness of the world is not going to stop Harry (even unconsciously, he can do magic), that we begin to cross the line and want to *be* him. When we find out he's a wizard, we commit wholeheartedly to the story.

Adult stories can use the same technique by showing the hero's past, his vulnerability as a child, something terrible that helped shape his character. The choices are nearly infinite.

WORKSHOP 28

WHO IS YOUR PROTAGONIST?

In every story, there is a protagonist and antagonist. The protagonist is usually the hero or heroine, the star of the story, the main character, the one around whom most of the action centers. The hero saves the day, or the world, at the end. The hero can also be an anti-hero, who loses in the end. Take Hamlet. After all he goes through to save his country and avenge his father, he dies unrewarded. (In *Hamlet*, we think the antagonist is the uncle, but in fact, it is death itself. Thus, because Hamlet is an anti-hero, all the main characters die at the end, not just the bad guy.)

Define your protagonist:

Who is your protagonist? What's his or her name?

What does he look like?

Where and when does he come from?

Has he ever been in love?

What happened to him when he was young that shaped who he is today?

Why should we care about him?

How does he speak? Does he have an accent? Is he abrupt, long-winded, quiet, shy, etc.?

What kinds of clothes does he wear?

Before he got involved in your plot, what did he dream of becoming?

Does he have any special skills or strengths?

Is he handicapped or weak in any way? What's his fatal flaw*?

What are his quirks?

Describe the house he grew up in and important relationships to his family.

What is his greatest fear?

What does he love the most?

Would he ever kill, and if so for what reason?
Do you care for this character? What does he mean to you?

Will the events of the plot change him? If so, how?

Is the hero truly heroic? What character traits define him as heroic?

What traits make him non-stereotypical? How is he unique and different from any other hero or heroine you've encountered?

Make a page in your notebook for the hero and write down as many answers to these questions as you can, or use the forms provided in the back of this book.

WORKSHOP 29

WHO OR WHAT IS YOUR ANTAGONIST?

The antagonist is the enemy, that which the hero must overcome, or that which the anti-hero must fight in his attempt to win. The antagonist can be a disease, a war, or any other event; or it can simply be a person on the other side. The antagonist can be evil personified (even glorified), or it can be a flawed character whom we understand, even as we reject him and all he stands for. The power of the antagonist defines the strength and determination of the hero, so you must make him a worthy adversary. The more powerful the antagonist, the more heroic the hero has to be to win against him.

Now ask yourself the same questions about your antagonist that you asked about the protagonist. Write down your answers in your notebook or use the Antagonist form in the back of the book.

Who is your antagonist?

What does he, she, or it look like?

Where does he come from?

Has he ever been in love? What happened?

What happened to him when he was young that shaped who he is today?

Do we care about him? If so, why? And when do we stop caring?

How does he speak? Is he smooth, abrupt, long-winded, whiny? Does he speak in clichés?

What does he wear?

Before he got involved in your plot, what did he dream of becoming?

Does he have any special skills or strengths?

Is he handicapped or weak in any way?

What are his quirks?

Describe the house he grew up in and his relationships to his family.

What is his greatest fear?

Does he love anything? What is his saving grace?

Why does he kill?

Describe a scene in which the antagonist appears:

Will the events of the plot change him? If so, how will he change?

Is your antagonist powerful enough to show us how strong your hero is?

Is the antagonist so powerful that we fear that the hero can't win? In what way?

What traits make your antagonist non-stereotypical? How is he unique?

How can you make your antagonist even stronger and more fearsome?

WORKSHOP 30

WHO IS YOUR LOVE INTEREST?

The love interest is often a person whom the hero and the antagonist (or an agent of the antagonist) both desire, or one whom the hero desires and the antagonist wants to hurt. The function of the love interest is often to be pulled apart by the protagonist and antagonist.

The love interest usually plays a significant role in the story, and is frequently the hero's reward for success. As the protagonist and antagonist vie for supremacy, the love interest becomes a physical manifestation of the conflict between them. How she (or he) fares is evidence of who's winning at any given time. When the love interest is captured by the villain, the hero is losing. When he recaptures her, he's winning.

Of course, not every story is an action movie. If the antagonist were a disease, then the love interest would surely have to succumb at some time and either be saved by the hero or lost to the scourge. If the antagonist were a hurricane, the love interest might have to be rescued at the height of the storm.

The love interest doesn't have to be a person. In *National Treasure*, although there was a woman who was a love interest, the real love was the treasure.

DEFINE YOUR LOVE INTEREST:

Who is your love interest?

What does he/she look like?

Where does he/she come from?

Has he/she ever been in love before? What happened?

What happened when he/she was young that shaped who he/she is today?

Do we care about him/her? If so, why?

How does he/she speak?

What does he/she wear?

Before he/she got involved in your plot, what did he/she dream of becoming?

Does he/she have any special skills or strengths?

Is he/she handicapped or weak in any way? What are his/her flaws?

What are his/her quirks?

Describe the house he/she grew up in and his/her relationships to family.

What is his/her greatest fear?

Does he/she love the hero?

Is he/she capable of killing?

Describe a scene in which the love interest appears:

Will the events of the plot change him/her? If so, how will he/she change?

What traits make your love interest non-stereotypical? How is he or she unique?

Use the form in the back of the book or make a page in your notebook for the love interest and write down as many answers to these questions as you can.

WORKSHOP 31

SUPPORTING CHARACTERS

Besides agents and sidekicks, you will need other supporting characters, sounding boards, people who advance the plot. Beware of characters who have the exact same motivation and beliefs as other characters (especially if you're fictionalizing your life in some way). In dramatic terms, these are the same character, so get rid of duplicates. All characters should have a set of beliefs, motivations, and needs that are uniquely theirs, and every character must behave according to his character.

You can't have someone hold up your hero and demand money unless that character has it in him. Readers won't tolerate lying from the author, so you must create real characters who act according to their needs, while at the same time performing their roles in your drama. For example, say you have a character who dreams about getting a new car. You can't suddenly make that character walk away from the opportunity because you need him to do something else (unless self-sacrifice is also part of his character). Or say you have a character whose only real function is to listen to the hero talk. If you don't give that person a motivation and something to say, he or she will be wooden and flat—boring.

Characters must be three-dimensional, meaning they must have a history, needs, and desires. You don't need to, and shouldn't, tell us all the details about every character, but to make sure that characters are three-dimensional and true to themselves, *you* should have some sense of what those details are. If it's a really minor character, one who makes an appearance and disappears, you may need no more than a description, a name, and a quirky characteristic, but you should explore the background of every major character.

Characters have a place in the story. The hero may have a sidekick or friend who supports him in times of trouble and adds a little humor in the midst of flying debris and exploding bombs. This is almost always done in action movies, but not always in novels. The antagonist may have an underling who functions as a sounding board, or he may have an agent who shows just how evil the antagonist really is by carrying out his orders in all their gory detail. A character can take a particular philosophical perspective in a story that questions a moral issue. For instance, if we were to create a novel questioning the death penalty, we might have one character who's all for it and another who's completely against it. And we might also have a character who's about to be subject to it.

Ask these questions about each of your supporting characters. Take your time and write down your answers for each character.

Who is your character, and what is his main function in the story?

What does he (she or it) look like?

Where does he come from?

Has he ever been in love? What happened?

What happened to him when he was young that shaped who he is today?

Do we care about him? If so, why? Do we stop caring? If so, why?

How does he speak? Is he smooth, abrupt, long-winded, whiny? Does he speak in clichés?

What does he wear?

Before he got involved in your plot, what did he dream of becoming?

Does he have any special skills or strengths?

Is he handicapped or weak in any way?

What are his quirks?

Describe the house he grew up in and his relationships to his family.

What is his greatest fear? What's his fatal flaw or saving grace?

What does he want and desire?

If he has to kill, what could make him do such a thing?

Will the events of the plot change him? If so, how will he change?

What can you do to make this character more (or less) sympathetic?

NOTE: Remember, in all these exercises, your final decisions will be based on instinct. That is, does the idea, the thought, the character, or what happens to the character create an echo of the dramatic moment within you? Does this or that *feel* right? Does it satisfy? Or do you feel okay about it, but feel something nagging at you (sometimes in a barely perceptible way) to go back and think about it again? Follow your instincts; they are your surest guide.

WORKSHOP 32

AGENTS AND SIDEKICKS

Antagonists have agents, people or things they use to help achieve their goals, and protagonists have sidekicks. These characters act in lieu of hero and villain, and sometimes we don't know right away that the antagonist the hero is fighting is merely an agent.

AGENTS

The agents of the antagonist are the henchmen: the troops of the dictator, the demon who carries out the orders of the Satan, the government scientists who are unwilling to take the necessary risks to stop the plague. The agent is the one who does the work of the antagonist. When he (or it) is defeated, the hero will have to stop the antagonist himself. For instance, in the movie, *The Fifth Element*, Bruce Willis's character, Korbin Dallas, is sent to a space resort to retrieve the stones needed to defeat the absolute evil that is threatening the world. Also in search of the stones are a band of alien thugs hired by Zorg (the antagonist's agent on earth). Even though Bruce defeats the thugs and Zorg and blows up the space resort, it's not enough. The real antagonist is stopped on earth's doorstep with only seconds to spare. When the agent is killed, the hero will have to deal directly with the bad guy himself.

Agents are not always willing workers for the antagonist. They can simply be cowardly or ignorant rather than evil. For example, suppose the hero is trying to save his land from a flood and the neighbors won't help for fear of the man who's waiting on the sidelines to buy up the devastated property. The neighbors are not evil, but they are afraid. This makes them useful as agents of the bad guy.

SIDEKICKS
Not all heroes have sidekicks, but many do. Sidekicks have many uses. They can act as sounding boards, listening to the hero's plans, and helping the author develop the character. Sidekicks can also help the hero to implement his plans when the time comes. They can sometimes act as a go-between, taking the messages of the hero to the enemy. Sometimes, they can be captured and used to carry messages to the hero.

A classic sidekick is Sancho Panza in *Man of La Mancha*. He listens; he helps his master out of trouble when he tilts at windmills; he helps smooth the way before people who don't understand Don Quixote's idealistic insanity.

Another memorable sidekick is Horatio in *Hamlet*. He acts as friend, as confidante, and when Hamlet dies, he is the witness who will remember.

Ron Weasley in Harry Potter acts as Harry's sidekick in both book and movie.

Don't confuse a co-hero with a sidekick. Luke Skywalker and Han Solo are both heroes, although you may doubt it at first. R2D2 and 3CPO on the other hand, are sidekicks.

In books, it may be more difficult to identify these

characters than it is in movies, but they are there. In Terry Pratchett's *The Color of Magic*, the inept wizard/hero, Rincewind, has two: the unique tourist, Twoflower, and the Luggage, which takes on a life of its own.

Exercise:

Here are some movies you may have seen:
Diehard
Braveheart
Legally Blonde
Spiderman
Superman

Pick one or two of these films and identify the hero, the villain, the love interest, and any agents or sidekicks and their functions. Write down your observations in your workbook.

WORKSHOP 33

MINOR CHARACTERS

There will be many minor characters in your book. Some you may invent on the spur of the moment, and some you'll already know about. Some writers find it useful to have a few different types sitting around waiting to be called on stage. If they've already got names, characteristics, and minor fleshing out, they can quickly be called into action before you "lose the light" while searching for a name. Take a few moments to create some of the characters you think you might need. These could be errand boys, delivery or shop personnel—the list is long. It's important to give even minor characters names.

Try to answer these questions for each of the minor characters you develop.

Minor Character Name:
Description:
Age:
Sex:
Quirk:
Purpose in story:

WORKSHOP 34

CHARACTER IS DESTINY

There is a difference between character and personality. Personality is what we show the world, how we behave in our social relationships, the little quirks that endear us to others or that make them hate us. She's always biting her nails; he never shuts up; she sings while she works; he speaks with a lisp. These are examples of personality traits. They are the veneer created by society or for society, the ways we deal with the world in which we live. They may tell us a person is nervous or content, or whether they need dental work, but they don't tell us whether a person is good or bad, cowardly or brave, determined or flighty. They tell us nothing about how an individual will behave when the world begins to fall apart.

Character is what lies within, sometimes deep inside, often unknown even to the character. It's the person we really are, the sum of our genetic inheritance and the hard won lessons of life, as opposed to the assumed traits of personality. When terrorists bomb buses and loved ones fall into the line of fire, we see what an individual is really made of. This is character. Who the characters truly are will determine what they do. If a character is a timid soul who can't swim, it's very unlikely he'll jump in a raging river to save the damsel in distress. But your hero can look timid because he's really just a quiet guy who doesn't like to fight, and when circumstances warrant, his hidden strength can come out. It's crucial that you understand the motivations and the essential being of your characters so that you can show them accurately and keep the people who inhabit your world "in character."

Some writers believe that circumstance can change character, that plot influences who the character is and how he reacts, and that plot will alter that character in the end. That makes sense. People do learn, don't they? Other writers believe that character never changes, that hidden character traits can be revealed, but if it's not there to begin with, it won't suddenly appear. This is something you will have to decide for yourself and for your characters.

Exercises:

Who are some of the characters who will people your book? Give each character a page in your notebook and write a brief description of each of them and the personality and character traits that mark them.

Now, take out a sheet of paper and write a short summary of your novel. (Example: *Unable to cope, Judy sets out to make the world aware of the injustices heaped upon her son. In the process come healing, forgiveness, and a new beginning. Based on a true story,* Mirror, Mirror *deals with individuals lost in a maze of social expectations and reflections.*)

Don't worry if you can't do that yet. Sometimes, you have to write the whole book before you can sum it up in a couple sentences. For some writers, a short summary is harder than writing the book.

WORKSHOP 35

ANALYZE PLOT AND CHARACTER

Characters work within the plot to create the substance of the book. The conflicts between the characters, or between the protagonist and an antagonist set the plot in motion. In a plot driven work, the plot drives the action. Something must happen, so the characters must be bent to the plot.

In a character driven work, it's the opposite. Since character is destiny, the internal workings of the character drive the plot. In many works, it's a little of both. Neither is more right than the other. There are readers for both types. However, it is important for you, as the author, to know which is your preference, and to work out details of plot and character so that it all works for you.

Exercises:

Analyze your characters in terms of the plot and write down your thoughts in your notebook. Consider each of the major characters as he or she interacts with the plot. These questions are a good starting point:

1. Do the characters exist to advance the plot?
2. Do you have "good" and "bad" characters? A protagonist and antagonist?
3. Can the protagonist be more sympathetic? How?
4. Can you make the antagonist more fearsome?

5. Does the reader understand where each character is coming from and why he is who he is?
6. Are the characters believable?
7. Does the reader like the ones he's supposed to like and dislike those he's supposed to dislike?

GOD IS IN THE DETAILS

Albert Bierstadt, *Looking Down Yosemite Valley, California* (1865)
(Author's note: It's better in color!)

WORKSHOP 36

DIALOGUE

Dialogue should sound like real speech, although it really isn't because all the boring bits have been left out. In real life, people utter a lot of nonsense: Hi, how are you? Oh, fine, and you? Hey, I'm great. Isn't this great weather we're having? Oh, yes. But last year was much hotter, wasn't it? This is BORING. Never bore your reader with dialogue that does not tell us something about the character or advance the plot in some way. Dialogue should sound natural to the ear, but it usually takes a lot of work on the part of the writer to make it sound that way.

Different characters will speak in different ways. Some will be straightforward and some will beat around the bush. Some will be articulate, and others will have to have every word dragged out of them. One technique you can use is to match your characters to people you really know. Though they may be completely unlike the real person you're using, if they talk like him or her, you can try to catch the cadence and patterns of real speech in what they say. I know someone who speaks almost exclusively in metaphor, and if I have a character I want to be mysterious and unknowable, I think of how this person speaks. Or I know another man who's a lawyer and everything he says is direct and to the point, even blunt. When I have a character who is like that, I think of how this person talks.

You can write dialects if you want, but be careful. Many readers don't like them because they're hard to read, and they're hard to write consistently, as well. If you want to flavor the speech of a character with dialect, then choose a few words to do it with. For instance, instead of saying, "Yawl're alus gonna be welcum heah," it's preferable to imply the accent with a few well-chosen words in correct, if not perfect, English: "You all are always gonna be welcome here." "You all" and "gonna" gives us the sense that the accent is southern, and that's all the reader needs.

Terry Pratchett is a master storyteller, and he does dialogue that is stunningly individual. Every character speaks in their own way with their own cadences, metaphors, and patterns. In *Carpe Jugulum*, however, he introduces the wee free men, a tribe of pictsies (spelling his) and the dialogue was so difficult to read, I was almost disappointed. (Don't worry, he makes up for it in other ways, and the book is still great.) In future novels featuring these wee free men, however, he tones the dialogue down a bit, and it works perfectly. In fact, you get to love them.

When you were working on your characters, you may have already filled in ideas on how each one speaks. Now, go back and look at them again. What do you want to change?

1. Where is the character from?
2. Do people from that place have a recognizable way of speaking?
3. What kind of slang is appropriate to his or her age?
4. Does your character use buzzwords related to work or position in society?
5. How fast or slow does your character speak?

6. Does your character speak directly, or does he or she avoid getting to the point?
7. Does your character use metaphor? If so, what kinds would he use?

WORKSHOP 37

TIPS ON DIALOGUE

Dialogue not only needs to sound realistic, it has to accomplish certain tasks and avoid certain pitfalls:

- Dialogue creates immediacy and overcomes emotional distance. It pulls the reader into a scene in a way that exposition cannot. You should use dialogue in all your pivotal scenes.

- Never write small talk. It is boring.

- Don't preach through dialogue unless the character is a preacher-type who can't help it. No one likes to be lectured, especially not readers.

- Wherever dialogue can be used to intensify conflict, use it. For instance, if you've got two people who hate each other but haven't yet become violent, you can use dialogue to show their feelings. Remember *War of the Roses*? He said, "I love you." And she said, "I hate you." They both said exactly what they meant, but he wouldn't believe her. What if it had been written, "'I love you, too," she said, but really didn't mean it. Boring.

- The word "said" is largely invisible. So use it when needed and avoid using phrases like "she replied, she offered, he suggested, he added, she remarked," which all mean "said." These words draw attention to themselves but rarely add much in the way of plot or character development. Also, carefully consider using words that describe body language as part of dialogue: "she laughed, he smirked." These are actually actions that should be shown as action, not speech. For instance, compare these two scenes:

USING REPLACEMENTS FOR "SAID" INSTEAD OF ACTION

Judy strolled through the crowd around the pool, the end of summer festivities flowing all around her. Although she'd tried to avoid him, her father's raspy voice caught her in mid-stride, and she shivered with cold that had nothing to do with the weather.

"Judy," he said. "You really know how to throw a party."

"Thanks, Dad," she smiled. "That's high praise from someone who's dined at the White House."

"Ah, don't make so much of it," he responded. "I'm just another soldier."

"Oh, is that soldier of fortune or fighting soldier? Mercenary? What kind of soldier would that be?" she smirked

"Oh, probably the kind that steals women and demands tribute," he laughed.

"Like a Roman soldier. How like you, Daddy. Conquest always was in your blood."

"Winning is like a drug. Better than sex. Better than—"

Thank God, she was saved from hearing what else it was better than by David's greeting.

USING ACTION INSTEAD OF REPLACEMENTS FOR "SAID"

Judy strolled through the crowd around the pool, the end of summer festivities flowing all around her. Although she'd tried to avoid him, her father's raspy voice caught her in mid-stride, and she shivered with cold that had nothing to do with the weather.

"Judy," he said. "You really know how to throw a party."

The smile on her face felt pasted on. "Thanks, Daddy. That's high praise from someone who's dined at the White House."

He tipped his cocktail at her and donned his sheepish *I'm just one of the guys* look. "Ah, don't make so much of it. I'm just another soldier."

"Oh, is that soldier of fortune or fighting soldier? Mercenary? What kind of soldier would that be?"

His eyes glittered, predatory and dangerous. "Oh, probably the kind that steals women and demands tribute." He laughed and slipped his arm around his latest trophy wife.

Judy bit her lip and looked away. When would he die? "Like a Roman soldier. How like you, Daddy. Conquest always was in your blood."

"Winning is like a drug. Better than sex. Better than—"

Thank God, she was saved from hearing what else it was better than by David's greeting. Darling David, who actually liked the bastard who was her father.

Consider how much more we've learned about the characters from this exchange in comparison to the first one. Then write out one of your pivotal scenes in detail. Use the beginning, middle, and end technique we've already discussed and add in dialogue and action.

When you finish, go over your scene again and rewrite it. Condense dialogue; get rid of as many words as possible. Make sure the feelings you want to convey are in the spoken words or action, and that you're not supporting them with phrases like "he argued" instead of showing the argument in the words and action. When you're finished, answer this: What did you learn?

WORKSHOP 38

GROUNDING DIALOGUE

Have you ever heard of someone who was "all talk?" Some inexperienced writers put all the action of the story into the dialogue, making the book all talk, and it doesn't work. It tends to end up a bit surreal after a while as you read these long conversations that have no substance. Instead of creating a living, breathing scene that the reader can hear, smell, taste, visualize, and even touch, they create lengthy discussions that become very quickly very boring.

Although you can put a great deal of detail into the dialogue of your scenes, it's imperative to ground that dialogue. In other words, show what's going on around it. Where are your characters standing, sitting, moving to? What are they doing? What objects are they handling? What do they see or smell?

Let's see what happens if we take the grounding out of the previous scene:

> "Judy," her father said. "You really know how to throw a party."
> "Thanks, Daddy. That's high praise from someone who's dined at the White House."
> "Ah, don't make so much of it. I'm

just another soldier."

"Oh, is that soldier of fortune or fighting soldier? Mercenary? What kind of soldier would that be?"

"Oh, probably the kind that steals women and demands tribute."

"Like a Roman soldier. How like you, Daddy. Conquest always was in your blood."

"Winning is like a drug. Better than sex. Better than—"

What have we learned from this scene? Judy knows how to throw a party. Her father must be someone important, some kind of soldier, maybe a general?

We don't learn that it's the end of summer, that the party is outside around the pool, that Judy hates her father, and so much more.

WORKSHOP 39

SETUPS AND PAYOFFS

Things happen in stories, and sometimes you'll need for something else to be there already so that the action is believable. For instance, in the scene we discussed earlier, the fact that Evie found a nail scissors and a box of talcum powder in the bathroom is believable. Those things are kept in bathrooms, but what if she'd pulled a gun and shot him through the door. Where did the gun come from? Why is it in the bathroom? Why does a fourteen-year-old girl keep a gun in a place where doors are never locked? It's completely illogical.

However, let's say we want to use the gun. Is there no way we can do that? In fact, there is. All we have to do is *set up* the existence of the gun and the reasons it's in the bathroom earlier in the story. Suppose Evie had found it in a little-used corner of the habitat and secreted it in her bathroom because there was a panel behind which she could hide it. The gun may have had another purpose at that point, but now its real purpose is revealed as she pulls it out and shoots her assailant. This is the payoff.

Setups can involve anything. All writers have faced a moment like this at some time in their careers or seen it happen in a movie: The plot shows our hero (a smart, tough businesswoman) being attacked by the villain, but instead of turning him over to the police after she knocks him over the head with a tire iron and stops him in his tracks, she runs away and allows him to recover. This is ridiculous. However, because the plot requires that he come after her again, we, or some writer somewher decided that realism was less important than keeping the plot on track.

This may work on screen because we tend to believe when we see, but not in a book. Our readers are not ignorant and will resent the implication that they are. Still, we need to have the villain attack her again. The answer is to set up a reason why she, contrary to story logic, runs away. If we learned earlier that she panics at the sight of blood, we could understand her behavior. We set this up in an earlier scene and pay it off in this one.

Just remember, for every setup there has to be a payoff. Don't setup an object or a person to be used in a later scene and then fail to use it. The reader will wonder what happened and be unsatisfied if he's never told.

If you can, identify scenes that happen later in your story that need to be set up earlier. Look especially at pivotal scenes. Sometimes, you may just have to go back later and setup something that you felt was necessary.

WORKSHOP 40

CREATING SUSPENSE: DON'T FORGET THE CLIFFHANGERS AND COUNTDOWNS

When we first begin to read a work of fiction, we stay with it because we're curious. What's going on? Who are these people, and why should I be interested? When one question is answered, another should be introduced. Stop here and write down some of the questions you raise in your reader's mind during the beginning of your story (before the point of no return).

Once the story reaches the point-of-no-return scene (which we're also calling the kiss), the reader has to have had his curiosity satisfied in some ways and be so involved that he's now drawn into the suspense. Suspense is created when the reader doubts or is uncertain that the character will carry out the action as intended. For instance, in *Back to the Future*, suspense is created when Doc is killed in the point-of-no-return scene. Marty hurtles into the past; Doc is apparently dead. We have no idea how Marty will get back. Suspense is also created when the reader knows or suspects that something will happen of which the character is unaware: the killer is hiding in the closet; there's an evil spell on that pretty little toy.

Another method of creating suspense throughout the book is a countdown. We've all seen countdowns in the movies: the clock is ticking; the bomb is going to go off. Everything focuses on that countdown until the final second, when all is saved or not. Countdowns usually happen during the climactic scene, but they don't have to. You can use them wherever you need to, and they don't all have to deal with ticking bombs. Think of Jim Carrey's son in *Liar Liar*, waiting for the six o'clock appearance of his father, who doesn't make it.

Creating cliffhangers is different. They happen throughout the book. In my first book, *The Healer*, I neatly finished every scene before going on to the next, so the reader knew that the boy fell from the cliff, but didn't die. When I read it over the tenth or eleventh time, I realized I was doing exactly the opposite of what I should be doing. Rewriting the whole thing with this understanding, I ended all chapters with the hero figuratively (and sometimes literally) hanging in space. Then I moved on to another scene and another character. When I came back to the hero hanging in space, I let him down and relieved the reader of the suspense of not knowing whether he survived, but I had left the last character in a similar quandary. Thus by bouncing from one state of fear, anticipation, or stark terror to the next, the reader is kept in a constant state of suspense. This is what makes a page-turner.

What will happen in your point-of-no-return scene to create suspense in the mind of the reader? Although he's committed to the action, the reader has to have reason to doubt he'll succeed.

Think about other pivotal scenes. Right after the middle of each of these scenes, at the climactic moment, break off the scene and tend to some other character. Your readers will not be able to put the book down until they find out what happened in that pivotal scene. If you can interweave scenes so that this happens frequently, you will be on your way toward that page-turner.

Going back to each pivotal scene, find and describe the cutoff place that will leave the reader in suspense.

WORKSHOP 41
FORESHADOWING

Foreshadowing, like cliffhangers, keeps readers involved. While cliffhangers usually come at the end of a scene and leave out the results of the action so that the reader has to keep reading in order to find out what happened, foreshadowing works a little differently.

Foreshadowing can be as simple as a single line indicating that something is about to happen, usually something bad or serious. Foreshadowing can come at the end of a scene, making the reader want to at least read the next paragraph, the next scene, or the next chapter. It can also come at the beginning of a paragraph, scene or chapter, grabbing the reader's interest and making him want to continue reading. Some examples are:

"I want to tell you about Bill," she said, to my utter surprise. "Bill, and Eric." From *All Together Dead* by Charlaine Harris. This little sentence comes at the end of a chapter and does its job admirably. The reader knows that the heroine has slept with both these men, and has to keep reading to find out what's up.

"For a moment, Mariam heard Nana's voice in her head, mocking, dousing the deep-seated glow of her hopes." From *A Thousand Splendid Suns* by Khalid Hosseini. This line is at the beginning of the final scene in a chapter, and it sends a shiver through the reader. We know something bad is going to happen, and must keep reading to find out more.

"Six minutes from now, one of us would be dead. That was our fate. None of us knew it was coming." This is the first line in *The Book of Fate* by Brad Meltzer, and it certainly does its job.

"Hatsumomo smiled when she was happy, like everybody else; and she was never happier than when she was about to make someone suffer." From *Memoirs of a Geisha*, this line sets the stage for the painful scene that is to come.

Exercises:

Go through some of your favorite books and find some lines that foreshadow the action.

Write some lines for your pivotal scenes that hint at what's coming just enough to keep the reader hooked.

WORKSHOP 42

WRITING DESCRIPTIONS

There is one rule here that should never be broken: Never interrupt the momentum to introduce a description. If you've got the reader hooked and want him to stay hooked, you need to keep him involved. Descriptions of setting and place are usually static and give the reader a chance to put the book down. To prevent this from happening, descriptions should be incorporated into the action. For example, you could stop the action to describe the long-legged blonde with swinging hair in detail, or you can tell us what she looks like in the midst of the action: Her long blond hair shifted to the side as she glanced his way. Okay, we worked that in. How about the long legs, full breasts, big blue eyes, and crooked grin? Talk about their meeting and work in her looks and his reaction to them while they talk.

> Her long blonde hair swung to the side as she glanced his way. Before Jake could catch his breath, he was on his feet and closing in. The scent of roses on her skin reached his nose before the rest of him reached her table. Was she waiting for someone?
>
> "Hi! I—I'm Jake. I couldn't help notice that you're sitting alone." He brushed his hand over his hair,

smoothing it, trying to make himself look less undone than he felt.

She probably thought he was an idiot. But those eyes, those lips: They made him ache. For a dizzy moment, he feared it would show.

"Yes," she said. "I am sitting alone. I actually like to sit alone."

"But I had to talk to you. You see, I'm a movie producer, and you look so perfect for this part we're casting." Oh, my God. What was he doing?

She smiled, crossing those long, silky legs. An image of them wrapped around his spine flashed across his mind.

"Really?" she said.

Jake shook the fog from his head. "No. Actually—no. I just thought you might let me join you if you thought I was someone important. Look. Let me start over. I'm Jake. I'm nobody, really." He groaned. Maybe he'd have to kill himself in a few minutes. Holding out what suddenly looked like a hairy paw, he knew all was lost.

But she studied it for a moment, then miraculously lifted a life-saving hand and grasped his. "Okay, Jake," she said. "Sit down."

We could work on this longer and work in the scene itself. The glow of candlelight on her skin, the contrast between her blue silk dress and the white tablecloth, the goblet of wine in her hand. The idea is to make the scene organic. Make it move. Make it live. Don't stop to do an inventory of her looks and the setting at the top and then move into the action. Make it all happen together.

A word about clichés: Don't use them. Of course, that whole scene as written above is a cliché, and I would never use it in a book, but the kinds of clichés I'm talking about are the ones we use all the time without thinking about them. They're the first automatic thought that comes to mind when we begin to write. We tend to think in phrases rather than single words and often come up with things like *came to blows, had a short fuse, was as dull as dishwater, roared like a lion, had eyes like sapphires, skin white as snow, moved as fast as a rocket.* Never use these types of phrases. They're old, worn out, boring metaphors. Instead, say what you want to say in a straightforward manner. *He was fast, and with proper training, there was no telling how much faster he'd run.* Or come up with a new and fresh metaphor: *He seemed to be set on fast forward. No one could outrun him.*

Use adjectives sparingly. You cannot strengthen a scene by adding more adjectives. It would not help to say the girl above had long, shiny blond hair, straight, smooth legs, and sapphire blue eyes. It wouldn't help to add that her lustrous, soft skin glowed incandescently or to say that her teeth were straight and well-shaped or that her face was oval with well-defined features and her breasts were round, sweetly curved, and full. Most of this is useless, so pick a few (two or three) adjectives and get the most you can out of them. In the previous scene, we used *long, blond* hair, *long, silky* legs, and a *life-saving* hand. That's all, but the reader can and will fill in the blanks.

Try not to use adverbs. Instead of using adverbs to

intensify a weak verb, use a stronger verb. For instance, instead of saying *he walked arrogantly*, say *he strode*. Say exactly what you mean and use the best possible word to encompass your meaning.

Hey, no one ever said writing was easy.

WORKSHOP 43

WRITING FOR CLARITY

Clarity. That's what it's all about. The purpose of writing is to communicate ideas, thoughts, images, feelings, experiences, and this has to be done accurately. Let there be no mistake regarding your meaning. At the beginning of this book, we discussed art in general and how one of the primary skills of the artist is to be able to see clearly. If you can't see clearly, there's no way you'll ever be able to describe what you see. So let's start with a sensory exercise. Taking a pivotal scene from your story, work it over using all five of your senses.

What do your characters see?
Write a concise but thorough description of the surroundings, so that you can "see" it. Describe colors, shapes, objects etc.

What do your characters hear?
Is there a wind whistling through trees or down the canyons created by the buildings? Do your characters hear water going by or the endless noise of cars on the highway?

What do your characters smell?
Is the air perfumed by gardenias? Is the rotting smell of a dumpster nearby? Does the lawn smell like it has just been mown? Is someone sweating and smelly? Has someone just eaten onions?

What do your characters touch?
Everything has a texture: the cool, smooth hardness of marble, the roughness of concrete, the silky feel of her stockings when she crosses her legs, the stickiness of honey, the cool of a rose petal.

What do your characters taste?
Besides food, everything has a taste too: the air can taste of gasoline, or death; her skin can taste of perfume; the rolls they were eating can taste burnt. Food can be delicious, but try to use more accurate words like sweet, savory, garlicky, salty.

WORKSHOP 44

CLARITY IN PIVOTAL SCENES

Now, let's go back to that same pivotal scene as written in the lesson on dialogue and rework it once again, this time using some of the sensory information derived from the previous exercise. Think about the words you use. Are they the most accurate words for what your characters are experiencing? Use your thesaurus. Are there words that describe it even better? For instance, you could say the character smells flowers, but it's more accurate to say he smells roses or the faintest scent of gardenia. You could say he smells death, but it may be more accurate to say he smells putrefaction and decay. Use the most accurate terms for the greatest clarity.

This holds true in all instances. It's more accurate to say he ambled (if that's what he did) rather than walked slowly. It's more accurate to say his Jello jiggled than it is to say his Jello shook. It's more accurate to say her eyes were blue as the Aegean Sea than it is to say they were as blue as sapphires (these are usually very dark blue and don't resemble blue eyes at all).

For every word, you know, there are still more that you don't. Increasing your vocabulary can only make you a better writer. Reading books will help, especially if you read on an eReading device with a dictionary function that allows you to look up words you don't know as you go along.

WORKSHOP 45

EMOTIONAL DISTANCE

In all your scenes, you want to create immediacy. By closing the emotional distance between the reader and the writer, making the reader feel instead of think about what's going on, the writer creates immediacy. Consider these examples:

    1. It was the summer of 1978. Mary Baxter was uncomfortable in the heat.

    2. Mary Baxter detested the midsummer heat. She always had.

    3. Mary hated the sweat soaking through her shirt.

    4. Heat. Humidity. Sweat welling up between my breasts, dropping into my eyes, squelching in my shoes. I hate summer.

As you can see, the emotional distance decreases from one sentence to the next. If we're far away from the action, it's going to be hard to make us care. It's just the same as if you saw a man stealing a handful of bills from another man, but they're across the street in the middle of Manhattan. There's nothing you can do. But if it's happening in front of you, that's a whole different story. You can feel that story and get involved. What if it's so close that it's happening to you, or you're inside the mind of the person it's happening to? That's immediacy.

In fiction, emotional distance is like the wide, medium, and close shots of film. When we're far away, we can see the big picture. Then we get closer and see the most important parts of the big picture (what's happening to the main characters). Then we get very close and see into his eyes, see the expression on his face, the beauty or ugliness of his character.

When we're watching a movie, we usually start with a wide angle establishing shot and move progressively closer. The same goes for fiction. Although we may start with a close or medium distance that brings us directly into the action, we then have to back out and establish our location in time and space. Introduce characters and slowly move closer. The degree of immediacy will depend on the purpose of the scene. If it's a scene developing the characters and their motives, great immediacy might be called for, but if it's a scene showing a shipment of drugs coming in, we can experience this from a distance. Never mix up the degree of closeness within a scene. Readers cannot handle passages like *My God, right in front of him, not two feet away, they were fighting over a stack of bills. A fifty fluttered, and Bob dived after it, evading the kicking feet. The young man was used to doing what he wanted and getting his way in all things.*

In this short description, we went from a medium close shot to a wide shot (*The young man was used to doing what he wanted...*), and it *is* disconcerting. Pivotal scenes should be close and immediate, but you'll need to make a decision about the emotional distance you want to create in the mind of the reader in other scenes.

Besides its use in getting close to a character, immediacy can also be invoked by creating a situation in which the reader feels that something is going to happen. This forces the characters to make decisions and keeps the reader involved. This sense of impending change (whether that's a disaster in the making, a romantic meeting around the corner, or a confrontation that's long overdue), immediacy in this sense is a powerful tool.

WORKSHOP 46

PACING AND MOMENTUM

When we read, words flow from the author and into us. Well-written sentences are well-written because they don't interrupt this flow with awkward phrases or mistakes in grammar. They keep up a rhythm or pace that carries us along like a river carrying a leaf.

There are many analogies we could use to describe this pacing. We could imagine the river speeding up a bit as it goes around a curve, and then dancing along as the riverbed drops and we hit the rapids. Or we could go back to our roller coaster and include the speed of the coaster as part of the invisible structure of emotional ups and downs. Since we already noted the sexual nature of fiction, we can continue that metaphor as the relationship between author and reader and between hero and adversary moves along, slowly at first, and then speeding up as the participants approach the mini-climaxes of each scene.

When the pace is slow, you run the risk of boring your reader, but on the other hand, if the pace is too fast, you can exhaust him. Where is the happy medium? How do you decide on whether the pace should be slow or fast? How do you set the pace?

Here are a few suggestions for speeding up the pace:

1. Action. When things are happening, the pace quickens.

2. Use a tight focus on the scene. If you were using film, the scene would be in close up, and there would be little emotional distance between the reader and the people in the story. Show the character pressed against the wall trying not to breathe rather than the killer appearing across the street. Or use them both. For a quick pace, cut back and forth.

3. Use short, straightforward sentences. Pace will increase as sentences grow shorter and more direct, so leave out adverbs and adjectives when you want to quicken the pace.

4. Keep the dialogue short and snappy. This is not the time to discuss anything but what's going on in the scene.

There are also ways to slow down the pace. You can slow it down by stopping the action to explain the science behind your warp drive, or the reason birds migrate every winter. You can slow it down by digging into your characters' pasts, or by taking the time to describe the scenery. Here are a few suggestions for slowing the pace:

1. Slower scenes involve little or no action.

2. The camera (if this were a movie) would be set for a wide angle. Thse are the

scenes that provide description and exposition.

3. Use longer sentences with more adjectives and adverbs. Don't, however, go overboard. You should always be careful not to overuse them.

4. If you're using dialogue in slower scenes, this could be where you explore who the characters are and why they are that way.

Whatever the pace of the story as a whole, variety is the spice of life. Don't bore your reader with pacing that doesn't change. Intersperse slower scenes with faster ones, and be sure to let your reader take a breather between action scenes.

Exercises:

Go back to your pivotal scenes and the structure of feeling you created and examine your highs and lows. Make a note of the kinds of language you'll use in each of these places. Decide whether you should be using a close up scene or a distant one. Jot down ideas on writing these scenes.

WORKSHOP 47

ON BEING A GOD

I put the article "a" into the title lest your head get too big. However, it can't be helped; there is something god-like in writing. We create worlds and people and set them in motion, and we get so wrapped up in our creations that we sometimes forget to eat, to sleep, or to talk to other people. We're all alone; we're all that exists; we make people live; and we decide when they die. It's great.

The truth is, however, that once you create a character and a situation, that character may take on a life of his or her own. You may find that even though you thought you had it all under control, you miscalculated somewhere, and now your story is not going the way you expected and planned. Instead of heading out to sea to be lost in the hurricane waiting offstage, your character has decided he needs to stay on shore in case the love interest needs him. This can throw a monkey wrench into all your carefully constructed devices. What to do? What to do?

This is the time to remember that you aren't really a god. You may have created the character, but if the character is strong enough to have desires other than those you expected, that's a good thing. Characters have free will just like we do. Go with it. Find a way to let the character go his own way, but keep a tight enough rein that you don't get lost in a tangent. In the example above, where my hero was supposed to get lost in a hurricane at sea, I'll have to do some serious thinking to find a way to keep the story going where it's supposed to go, yet allow him to stay onshore to care for his lady love. Oh, I know. Maybe he can be washed out to sea while heading for her house. That works. He can stay true to character, I can still do what I want with him, and best of all, it adds drama and excitement to the story.

It's a delicate balance, and you always have to stay on top of it. Characters that come alive, that live up to the motivations and traits you've given them should be as unfettered as possible, but since you don't want to lose touch with your plot, you have to always keep it in mind, like cowboys keeping cattle from straying too far.

WORKSHOP 48

WRITE A TREATMENT

Okay. You've done a lot of the structural work. Now it's time to start putting it all together. A treatment is used in screenwriting, but it also works for other forms of dramatic fiction. A treatment is a short outline of each of the scenes in your story. It should be at *least* twelve to twenty pages, single-spaced, showing all the main plot points, the pivotal scenes, and the transitional scenes. Just tell what happens first and what happens next. Include flashbacks where you want them. If a scene comes to mind full-blown, write it out. Otherwise, just sketch it in.

Some authors prefer an outline. You should do whatever works best for you. I prefer the treatment because it's less structured and leaves me more room to develop ideas. At this stage, some scenes may come to you almost complete. You'll hear dialogue and see important details in your mind's eye. The treatment allows you to use everything without worrying about the structural requirements of an outline.

If you want, you can combine both these techniques in a more structured treatment, which outlines in places and includes scenes in others. Start with your opening scene and see what works for you.

If you're using the forms in the back of the book, or if

you've created your own, now is the time to put all your events in order and even lay them out on the floor or the wall on a timeline. Keep your character info in front of you, and get ready to write. You've already done a lot of this work in various exercises in this book, so you've got all the materials, and if you get stuck, you can refer to your scenes, characters, and pivotal scenes, so that you'll know what happens next.

If you haven't been using index cards or the forms provided, then you should start by organizing the material in your notebook.

Using the first form, your pivotal scene for the inciting event, begin writing the scenes in your treatment. It should look something like this:

It's the end of winter; everything is still grey. Diana jumps out of her mother's car and runs into the house. Her mother, Isabel, yells at her to get ready, go pack her bag. In the doorway, she gets into an argument with her twin brother, Eric, about the pending vacation. He doesn't believe they'll leave on time.

Just like that. Start the story. Describe each scene in as much detail as you can. If bits of dialogue come to mind, write them down. If a clever bit of foreshadowing comes to mind, make a note of it. Put everything you've got so far into the treatment, and make it as clear as possible. Don't worry too much about turning out perfect sentences at this point or about whether your metaphors are clichés. This is the time to get the basic structure of the book on paper.

If you get stuck, here are the magic words: What happens next?

WORKSHOP 49

ANALYZE WHAT YOU'VE GOT

Before you go on to this step, put your treatment aside for a few days. Work on something else. Go to the movies. Get away from the computer and go out with your friends. Although you may be in a great hurry to finish this book, this is a time to let it gestate. When you've relaxed sufficiently (and only you will know when that is), go back to your desk, pick up your printed treatment and take it somewhere else. You can take it to the dining room table, the library, to Starbucks, or anywhere else that feels comfortable. The point is to remove yourself from your usual workplace. Bring a pen and your notebook.

Once you're comfortable, begin reading your treatment. As you read, make notes either on the treatment itself (if there's room) or in your notebook. Note changes you want to make, bits of information you left out, new dialogue you want to add. If you see a hole in the plot, stop and figure out how to fix it. If it means going back and changing an earlier scene, do that. If you see a plot point that needs to be set up, figure out where it needs to be set up and add it in. This is the advantage of a treatment over writing a first draft. Because the treatment is short, you can go over it easily without getting lost in the details.

After you've gone over the treatment very carefully, go

back to the computer and type in your changes. Rewrite your treatment. Fill in missing information. Check for curiosity, pacing, and momentum. Did you leave out just enough information in the beginning to make the reader curious? Is the reader always wondering about what will happen next? Where will you foreshadow future events? Where will you leave cliffhangers?

Go over the second printed treatment as stringently as you did the first. This time ask yourself some serious questions: Does your beginning grab the reader's attention? Or can it be developed more fully? Is there a strong middle with serious obstacles that have to be overcome? Do your obstacles get more and more difficult for the hero to handle? Have you satisfied your reader's need for closure or have you left him hanging. Does your plot hang together, or is it confusing? Is the climax at the end of the book, or have you put it in too soon? What subplots do you have? Do they work? Do they support and strengthen the main plot? What about the structure of feeling? Can you see it? Do you know what the reader will feel each step of the way? What needs to be changed?

The more questions you ask, the more clearly you will be able to see the story develop. Keep adding to the treatment; keep filling in details, and above all, keep asking questions. If you don't know what to ask, go back over the lessons you've worked on throughout this book and ask the questions you find within.

When there are no more questions and you're satisfied that your treatment works, it's time to write the first draft of your book.

WORKSHOP 50

COMMON ERRORS IN ENGLISH

Its/it's –
"Its" is the possessive of "it." – That is its toy.
"It's" is the contraction of "it is." – It's a boy.

Your/you're –
"Your" is possessive. – It's your house.
"You're" is a contraction of "you are." – You're nuts.

There/their/they're –
"There" indicates place. – It's over there.
"Their" is possessive. – That's their sofa.
"They're" is a contraction of "they are." - They're here.

Passive voice –
Sentences like this: The bucket was held in his hand.
Better like this: He held the bucket in his hand.

Punctuation –
Books use the *Chicago Manual of Style*, and any questions you have regarding punctuation can be looked up there.

Verb tense –
I won't even go into this here, but if you're not thoroughly familiar with the uses of simple past vs past perfect vs conditional vs all the rest, you must take a grammar course or find some other way to learn. One of the best and most enjoyable ways to learn is by reading, and I have included a list of some of my favorite writers in the back of this book chosen not just for their stories and style, but also for their use of the English language.

CHAPTER 51

RULES ON WRITING

This is a brilliant essay on writing that every writer should read at least once, and I included it here so you would read it before starting to actually write your book.

Mark Twain on *Cooper's Prose Style*

YOUNG GENTLEMAN: In studying Cooper you will find it profitable to study him in detail-word by word, sentence bv sentence. For every sentence of his is interesting. Interesting because of its make-up, its peculiar make-up, its original make-up. Let us examine a sentence or two, and see. Here is a passage from Chapter XI of *The Last of the Mohicans*, one of the most famous and most admired of Cooper's books:

> Notwithstanding the swiftness of their flight, one of the Indians had found an opportunity to strike a straggling fawn with an arrow, and had borne the more preferable fragments of the victim, patiently on his shoulders, to the stopping-place. Without any aid from the science of cookery, he was immediately employed, in common with his fellows, in gorging himself with this digestible sustenance. Magua alone sat apart, without participating in the revolting meal, and apparently buried in the deepest thought.

This little paragraph is full of matter for reflection and inquiry. The remark about the swiftness of the flight was unnecessary, as it w'as merely put in to forestall the possible objection of some over particular reader that the Indian couldn't have found the needed "opportunity" while fleeing swiftly. The reader would not have made that objection. He would care nothing about having that small matter explained and justified. But that is Cooper's way; frequently he will explain and justify little things that do not need it and then make up for this by as frequently failing to explain important ones that do need it. For instance he allowed that astute and cautious person, Deerslayer-Hawkeye, to throw his rifle heedlessly down and leave it lying on the ground where some hostile Indians would presently be sure to find it-a rifle prized by that person above all things else in the earth-and the reader gets no word of explanation of that strange act. There was a reason, but it wouldn't bear exposure. Cooper meant to get a fine dramatic effect out of the finding of the rifle by the Indians, and he accomplished this at the happy time; but all the same, Hawkeye could have hidden the rifle in a quarter of a minute where the Indians could not have found it.

Cooper couldn't think of any way to explain why Hawkeye didn't do that, so he just shirked the difficulty and did not explain at all. In another place Cooper allowed Heyward to shoot at an Indian with a pistol that wasn't loaded-and grants us not a word of explanation as to how the man did it.

No, the remark about the swiftness of their flight was not necessary; neither was the one which said that the Indian found an opportunity; neither was the one which said he struck the fawn; neither was the one which explained that it was a "straggling" fawn; neither was the one which said the striking was done with an arrow; neither was the one which said the Indian bore the "fragments"; nor the remark that they were preferable fragments; nor the remark that they were more preferable fragments; nor the explanation that they were fragments of the "victim"; nor the overparticular explanation that specifies the Indian's "shoulders" as the part of him that supported the fragments; nor the statement that the Indian bore the fragments patiently. None of those details has any value. We don't care what the Indian struck the fawn with; we don't care whether it was a, struggling fawn or an unstruggling one; we don't care which fragments the Indian saved; we don't care why he saved the "more" preferable ones when the merely preferable ones would have amounted to just the same thing and couldn't have been told from the more preferable ones by anybody, dead or alive; we don't care whether the Indian carried them on his shoulders or in his handkerchief; and finally, we don't care whether he carried them patiently or struck for higher pay and shorter hours. We are indifferent to that Indian and all his affairs.

There was only one fact in that long sentence that was worth stating, and it could have been squeezed into these few words-and with advantage to the narrative, too: "During the flight one of the Indians had killed a fawn and he brought it into camp." You will notice that "During the flight one of the Indians had killed a fawn and he brought it into camp," is more straightforward and business-like, and less mincing and smirky, than it is to say, "Notwithstanding the swiftness of their flight, one of the lndians had found an opportunity to strike a straggling fawn with an arrow, and had borne the more preferable fragments of the victim, patiently on his shoulders, to the stopping-place." You will notice that the form "During the flight one of the Indians had killed a fawn and he brought it into camp" holds up its chin and moves to the front with the steady stride of a grenadier, whereas the form "Notwithstanding the swiftness of their flight, one of the Indians had found an opportunity to strike a straggling fawn with an arrow, and had borne the more preferable fragments of the victim, patiently on his shoulders, to the stopping-place" simpers along with an airy, complacent, monkey-with-a-parasol gait which is not suited to the transportation of raw meat.

I beg to remind you that an author's way of setting forth a matter is called his style, and that an author's style is a main part of his equipment for business. The style of some authors has variety in it, but Cooper's style is remarkable for the absence of this feature. Cooper's style is always grand and stately and noble. Style may be likened to an army, the author to its general, the book to the campaign. Some authors proportion an attacking force to the strength or weakness, the importance or unimportance, of the object to be attacked; but Cooper doesn't. It doesn't make any difference to Cooper whether the object of attack is a hundred thousand men or a cow; he hurls his entire force against it. He comes thundering down with all his battalions at his back, cavalry in the van, artillery on the flanks, infantry massed in the middle, forty bands braying, a thousand banners streaming in the wind; and whether the object be an army or a cow you will see him come marching sublimely in, at the end of the engagement, bearing the more preferable fragments of the victim patiently on his shoulders, to the stopping-place. Cooper's style is grand, awful, beautiful; but it is sacred to Cooper, it is his very own, and no student of the Veterinary College of Arizona will be allowed to filch it from him.

In one of his chapters, Cooper throws an ungentle slur at one Gamut because he is not exact enough in his choice of words. But Cooper has that failing himself, as remarked in our first lecture. If the Indian had "struck" the fawn with a brick, or with a club, or with his fist, no one could find fault with the word used. And one cannot find much fault when he strikes it with an arrow; still it sounds affected, and it might have been a little better to lean to simplicity and say he shot it with an arrow.

"Fragments" is well enough, perhaps, when one is speaking of the parts of a dismembered deer, yet it hasn't just exactly the right sound-and sound is something; in fact sound is a good deal. It makes the difference between good music and poor music, and it can sometimes make the difference between good literature and indifferent literature. "Fragments" sounds all right when we are talking about the wreckage of a breakable thing that has been smashed; it also sounds all right when applied to cat's meat; but when we use it to describe large hunks and chunks like the fore and hindquarters of a fawn, it grates upon the fastidious ear.

"Without any aid from the science of cookery, he was immediately employed, in common with his fellows, in gorging himself with this digestible sustenance." This was a mere statistic; just a mere cold, colorless statistic; yet you see Cooper has made a chromo out of it. To use another figure, he has clothed a humble statistic in flowing, voluminous and costly raiment, whereas both good taste and economy suggest that he ought to have saved these splendors for a king, and dressed the humble statistic in a simple breechclout. Cooper spent twenty-four words here on a thing not really worth more than eight. We will reduce the statistic to its proper proportions and state it in this way: "He and the others ate the meat raw."

"Digestible sustenance" is a handsome phrase, but it was out of place there, because we do not know these Indians or care for them; and so it cannot interest us to know whether the meat was going to agree with them or not. Details which do not assist a story are better left out.

"Magua alone sat apart, without participating in the revolting meal" is a statement which we understand, but that is our merit, not Cooper's. Cooper is not clear. He does not say who it is that is revolted by the meal. It is really Cooper himself, but there is nothing in the statement to indicate that it isn't Magua. Magua is an Indian and likes raw meat.

The word "alone" could have been left out and space saved. It has no value where it is.

I must come back with some frequency, in the course of these lectures, to the matter of Cooper's inaccuracy as an Observer. In this way I shall hope to persuade you that it is well to look at a thing carefully before you try to describe it; but I shall rest you between times with other matters and thus try to avoid overfatiguing you with that detail of our theme. In *The Last of the Mohicans* Cooper gets up a stirring "situation" on an island flanked by great cataracts-a lofty island with steep sides--a sort of tongue which projects down stream from the midst of the divided waterfall. There are caverns in this mass of rock, and a party of Cooper people hide themselves in one of these to get away from some hostile Indians. There is a small exit at each end of this cavern. These exits are closed with blankets and the light excluded. The exploring hostiles back themselves up against the blankets and rave and rage in a blood-curdling way, but they are Cooper Indians and of course fail to discover the blankets; so they presently go away baffled and disappointed. Alice; in her gratitude for this deliverance, flings herself on her knees to return thanks. The darkness in there must have been pretty solid; yet if we may believe Cooper, it was a darkness which could not have been told from daylight; for here are some nice details which were visible in it:

> Both Heyward and the more tempered Cora witnessed the act of involuntary emotion with powerful sympathy, the former secretly believing that piety had never worn a form so lovely as it had now assumed in the youthful person of Alice. Her eyes were radiant with the glow of grateful feelings; the flush of her beauty was again seated on her cheeks, and her whole soul seemed ready and anxious to poor out its thanksgivings, through the medium of her eloquent features. But when her lips moved, the words they should have uttered appeared frozen by some new and sudden chill. Her bloom gave place to the paleness of death; her soft and melting eyes grew hard, and seemed contracting with horror; while those hands which she had raised, clasped in each other, towards heaven, dropped in horizontal lines before her, the fingers pointed forward in convulsed motion.

It is a case of strikingly inexact observation. Heyward and the more tempered Cora could not have seen the half of it in the dark that way. I must call your attention to certain details of this work of art which invite particular examination. "Involuntary" is surplusage and violates Rule 14. **All emotion is involuntary when genuine, and then the qualifying term is not needed; a qualifying term is needed only when the emotion is pumped-up and ungenuine. "Secretly" is surplus-age, too; because Heyward was not believing out loud, but all to himself; and a person cannot believe a thing all to himself without doing it privately. I do not approve of the word "seated" to describe the process of locating a flush. No one can seat a flush. A flush is not a deposit on an exterior surface, it is a something which squishes out from within.

I cannot approve of the word "new." If Alice had had an old chill, formerly, it would be right to distinguish this one from that one by calling this one the new chill; but she had not had any old chill, this one was the only chill she had had, up till now, and so the tacit reference to an old anterior chill is unwarranted and misleading. And I do not altogether like the phrase "while those hands which she had raised." It seems to imply that she had some other hands-some other ones which she had put on the shelf a minute so as to give her a better chance to raise these ones; but it is not true; she had only the one pair. The phrase is in the last degree misleading. But I like to see her extend these ones in front of her and work the fingers. I think that that is a very good effect. And it would have almost doubled the effect if the more tempered Cora had done it some, too.

A Cooper Indian who has been washed is a poor thing, and commonplace; it is the Cooper Indian in his paint that thrills. Cooper's extra words are Cooper's paint-his paint, his feathers, his tomahawk, his war whoop.

In the two-thirds of a page elsewhere referred to, wherein Cooper scored 114 literary transgressions out of a possible

115, he appeals before us with all his things on. As follows; the italics are mine-they indicate violations of Rule 14:**

In a minute he was once more fastened to the tree, *a helpless object of any insult or wrong that might be offered. So eagerly did every one now act, that nothing was said.* The fire was immediately lighted *in the pile, and the end of all was anxiously expected.* It was not the intention of the Hurons *absolutely* to destroy *the life of* their victim by *means of* fire. They designed merely to put his *physical* fortitude to the severest proofs it could endure, short of that extremity. In the end, they fully intended to carry his scalp into their village, but it was their wish first to break down his resolution, and to reduce him to *the level of* a complaining sufferer. With this view, the pile of brush *and branches* had been placed at a *proper* distance, one at which it was thought the heat would soon become intolerable, though *it might* not *be* immediately dangerous. *As often happened, however, on these occasions,* this distance had been miscalculated, and the flames *began to wave their forked tongues in a proximity to the face of the victim that* would have proved fatal in another instant had not Hetty rushed through the crowd, armed with a stick, and scattered the blazing pile *in a dozen directions.* More than one hand was raised to strike the *presumptuous* intruder to the earth; but the chiefs prevented the blows by reminding their *irritated* followers of the state of her mind. Hetty, herself, was insensible to the risk she ran; but, *as soon as she had performed this bold act, she* stood looking about her in frowning resentment, as if to rebuke the *crowd of attentive* savages for their cruelty.

"God bless you, dear*est sister*, for that brave and ready act," murmured Judith, *herself unnerved so much as to be incapable of exertion;* "Heaven itself has sent you on its holy errand."

Number of words, 320; necessary ones, 220: words wasted by the generous spendthrift, 100.

In our day, those 100 unnecessary words would have to come out. We will take them out presently and make the episode approximate the modern requirement in the matter of compression.

If we may consider each unnecessary word in Cooper's report of that barbecue a separate and individual violation of Rule 14, then that rule is violated 100 times in that report. Other rules* are violated in it. Rule 12, 2 instances; Rule 13, 5 instances; Rule 15, 1 instance; Rule 16, 2 instances; Rule 17, 1 or 2 little instances; the report in its entirety is an offense against Rule 18-also against Rule 16. Total score, about 114 violations of the laws of literary art out of a possible 115.* Let us now bring forward the report again, with the most of the unnecessary words knocked out. By departing from Cooper's style and manner, all the facts could be put into 150 words, and the effects heightened at the same time-this is manifest, of course-but that would not be desirable. We must stick to Cooper's language as closely as we can:

> In a minute he was once more fastened to the tree. The fire was immediately lighted. It was not the intention of the Hurons to destroy Deerslayer's life by fire; they designed merely to put his fortitude to the severest proofs it could endure short of that extremity. In the end, they fully intended to take his life, but it was their wish first to break down his resolution and reduce him to a complaining sufferer. With this view, the pile of brush had been placed at a distance at which it was thought the heat would soon become intolerable, without being immediately dangerous. But this distance had been miscalculated; the fire was so close to the victim that he would have been fatally burned in another instant if Hetty had not rushed through the crowd and scattered the

brands with a stick. More than one Indian raised his hand to strike her down, but the chiefs saved her by reminding them of the state of her mind. Hetty herself was insensible to the risk she ran; she stood looking about her in frowning resentment, as if to rebuke the savages for their cruelty.

"God bless you, dear!" cried Judith, "for that brave and ready act. Heaven itself has sent you on its holy errand." (And you shall have a chromo.)

Number of words, 220-and the facts are all in.

* Rule 12: "[The author shall] Say what he is proposing to say, not merely come near it." Rule 13: "Use the right word, not its second cousin."
Rule I5: "Not omit necessary details."
Rule 16: "Avoid slovenliness of form. "
Rule 17: "Use good grammar."
Rule 18: "Employ a simple and straightforward style."

**Of nineteen rules "governing literary art in the domain of romantic fiction, " which Mark Twain had listed in "Fenimore Cooper's literary Offenses" (in How to Tell a Story, 1897), and of which, he claimed, Cooper's Deerslayer violated eighteen. The fourteenth is "Eschew surplusage. "

Here's a useful exercise:

Look at the sample text above and find these violations of the rules:
    Rule 12, 2 instances
    Rule 13, 5 instances
    Rule 15, 1 instance
    Rule 16, 2 instances
    Rule 17, 1 or 2 little instances
    Figure out why the report in its entirety is an offense against Rule 18-and against Rule 16.

Mark Twain also says that, "by departing from Cooper's style and manner, all the facts could be put into 150 words, and the effects heightened at the same time." See if you can do it.

WORKSHOP 51

WRITING THE FIRST DRAFT

Using your treatment, write the first draft of the beginning of your book. This should include the first pivotal scene, the inciting event, and it should begin developing the main characters and setting up the events that will swing the plot into motion. It will end when the hero is committed to his role in the story. It can take as many chapters as you need.

Your first and primary purpose when opening the book, is to gain the interest of the reader. If they've turned the first page, you cannot let them get away. Make your first paragraph, and if possible your very first sentence, a grabber. For example, "I stared at the pink slip in my hand in disbelief." That's a grabber. It tells us a lot: the narrator has been fired, and he or she was not prepared for it. It also rouses our curiosity. Why was he fired? Did he not deserve it?

Or how about something like: "How was I to know that within a week, my best friend would be dead?"

Clearly, a line that foreshadows events to come is a good way to start a book, but this is just the first line. What next? Now you have to write a first paragraph that keeps those feelings of curiosity high as you move toward the inciting event. This scene, as we discussed before, is the event that initiates the plot. Using the first example above, we might begin with a scene showing the recipient of the pink slip going back to the window and grabbing the shirt of the clerk handing out the checks. Or he could track down the big boss. What's important is to create a scene.

I stared at the pink slip in my hand in disbelief. It took a moment for me to grasp it, but before I'd even had the time to imagine what Jenny would say, I was in motion, turned around and heading up the hall to Mr. Marshall's office.

His door was closed. Of course; it was always closed. No man of the people, this guy. I slammed it open and stood in the doorway, breathing hard. "You son of a bitch. What do you mean by this?" I said waving the pink slip under his nose. "I'm fired? You fired me?"

Marshall stood up. He'd better stand up because I was about to leap over the desk and take him apart. "Now Bill," he said. "Stay calm."

"Stay calm! I have kids, you bastard. What're my kids gonna eat?"

You get the idea. Use your pivotal scene treatment and outlines to design this event so that it satisfies its purposes. It should introduce the characters in action. It should rouse the reader's curiosity. It might foreshadow events to come of leave the reader with a cliffhanger. From there, proceed paragraph by paragraph, scene by scene to the next pivotal scene: the point of no-return.

WORKSHOP 52

ANALYZE THE LANGUAGE

Analyze the language of the first chapter. Go back over your first draft of the beginning of the book. Read it on the computer and look at it in terms of language. Look at grammar, sentence structure, and flow. Rewrite all awkward sentences; make sure transitions are clear and the sentences flow in logical sequence. If they're sequential, make sure the time order is clear. This is especially important if the story is told out of time sequence. In that case, make sure that you haven't confused your reader. Do they know not only what's going on, but when it's going on?

Do you overuse adjectives? Cut wherever you can, so that sentences and meaning is explicit wherever possible. If you want to hide things from the reader, don't do it by using unclear language. That doesn't work. Hide things by skillful construction, not by using poor English.

Can you cut out superfluous word? Use a hatchet. Do not spare your finest phrases. They may have been fun to write, but if the information isn't absolutely necessary to the exploration of character or advancement of plot, you probably don't need them.

Take out all instances of repetitiveness. Remember,

your readers are intelligent. Don't' beat them over the head with information. If you say something once and say it clearly, it should be sufficient.

I once had a job writing on-hold messages for business telephones, and it was the greatest training. Back then, the systems used a cassette tape rather than a CD or computer, and space was limited. This meant I had to keep my messages short and succinct, and since they were read aloud, they had to flow smoothly too. From this job, I learned three lessons that have been of inestimable value to me as a writer:

1) Cut ruthlessly. Unless a word is actively participating in the meaning and purpose of a sentence, get rid of it.

2) Make sure that sentences are varied. Do not use the same sentence structure over and over again. For instance, you could say, "He saw the newspaper on the table. He picked it up and read the headlines. He couldn't believe what was going on in the world." Or you could say the same thing this way: "He saw the newspaper on the table. Picking it up, he read the headlines. Were his eyes deceiving him? Was the world really in that much trouble?" Hear the difference?

3) Finally, read every word of your work out loud. When you read aloud, you hear the cadence and rhythm, how words fit together. Oftentimes, you'll hear things that you might miss just by reading.

WORKSHOP 53

ANALYZE THE STRUCTURE

Now that you've rewritten once for language, you'll find that fewer places catch you up. On this second rewrite, besides looking again for language that isn't quite right, read and analyze the structure.

Map out the structure of feeling on a line using your draft. Show where feelings should go up and where they fall off. Is this what you wanted to do, or did you have something else in mind? You can use arrows on your second draft to note where feelings go up or down, or don't change as they should. Review the chapter on the structure of feeling and see what you can do to push feelings further in the direction you want them to go. If you want intense feeling but aren't getting it, what can be altered? Can you use more dramatic language? Improve the scene itself?

Here are some questions you should ask yourself as you go through this rewrite:

Does your opening scene create curiosity and interest?

Do you introduce the main character in a way that makes the reader want to know more?

How quickly do you hook the reader?

Have you raised questions in the mind of the reader?

Are your descriptions of action clear and logical?

How can you improve this part of the book?

WORKSHOP 54

WRITE THE REST

Now that your beginning is off to a solid start, use your treatment to finish the book. Flesh out each of your scenes and add details as needed. Keep your character cards, forms, or whatever you've decided to use handy, so you can use what you've already developed.

If you've reached this stage and have been doing the work, then you should now be ready to write a creditable first draft of your novel. Although there will probably be many rewrites as you hone and refine your material, the prep work you've done will keep you on track, help you over the bumps, keep you from traveling far afield in search of your plot, and even prevent writer's block.

If you've gotten this far, you can do this, and now is the time to get going. Have fun!

WORKSHOP 55

IT'S DONE!

At last, you've written the first draft, and it's quite an accomplishment. Go out and celebrate. Oh yes, there's still a lot of work to be done, but getting this far took gumption and power, and you've done it. So now, stop for a while. Print out the whole thing and put it in your desk drawer for a later day.

It depends on the person, but I usually need a month or two between drafts. Others may be able to go back to it a week later. Go back to it after you've gotten re-involved with the people in your life. When the book is no longer the first thing you think of when you get out of bed and the last thing you think of before going to sleep, it's probably time to get it out of mothballs and take another look.

Writing is hard work. Like any creative endeavor, it drains you. Since no one wants to make a lot more work for themselves while they're already doing a lot of work, it's best to wait until you've recovered from the first creative labor before taking that manuscript out of the drawer, analyzing your work, and seeing what else has to be done. If you wait long enough, you can probably be more objective about it.

Try to read the manuscript as if you never saw it before,

as if it were all new to you, as if you were someone else. As this is your only your first draft, don't be surprised to find many mistakes. There may be scenes that belong somewhere else, and long informative or descriptive pages that can be eliminated. Look for holes in the plot, places where information should have been provided, but wasn't. Check your setups and payoffs. If you have to add in a setup to justify a later payoff, do that now. Check your pivotal scenes and make sure they're doing their jobs of turning the emotions of the reader and advancing the plot. As always, look for language that can be tweaked and made more clear, and if you find your mind wandering, (yes, it's possible) check to make sure you're not boring your reader.

When you've scribbled all over your pages, take the manuscript back to the computer and insert the changes. While you're doing that, you might as well read it analytically again, so that the next draft you print will actually be your third.

That's the process. You can ask someone who's a reader and who is not afraid to insult you to read it on the third or fourth draft. Try to listen to their suggestions without rancor, accepting those you can use and putting aside those you can't.

When it's been rewritten five or six times, you are probably ready to submit it to an agent or publisher.

I wish you all the best, and hope to see your work in print. ☺

Character and Scene Summaries

MAIN CHARACTER: **PROTAGONIST**

Name:		Age:	
Physical Characteristics	Bio	Personal Motivation	
Hair:			
Eyes:			
Height:			
Striking Features:			
		Heroic Qualities	

Distinctive Language:	Quirks:	Fatal Flaws:

NOTES:

SIDEKICK CHARACTER: (PROTAGONIST)

Name: **Age:**

Physical Characteristics	Connection to Protagonist	Personal Motivation
Hair:		
Eyes:		
Height:		
Striking Features:		
		Heroic Qualities
	Function on behalf of Protagonist	

Distinctive Language:	Quirks:	Fatal Flaws:

NOTES:

SUPPORTING CHARACTER: (**PROTAGONIST**)

Name: **Age:**

Physical Characteristics	Connection to Main Characters	Personal Motivation
Hair:		
Eyes:		
Height:		
Striking Features:		
		Heroic Qualities
	Function on behalf of Protagonist	

Distinctive Language:	Quirks:	Fatal Flaws:

NOTES:

MAIN CHARACTER: **ANTAGONIST**/ human

Name: **Age:**

Physical Characteristics	Bio	Personal Motivation
Hair:		
Eyes:		
Height:		
Striking Features:		
		Evil Qualities:

Distinctive Language:	Quirks:	Saving Grace:

NOTES:

MAIN CHARACTER: **ANTAGONIST**/ non-human			
Name:			
Physical Characteristics	Bio		Its Motivation
Hair:			
Eyes:			
Height:			
Striking Features:			
			Qualities:

Distinctive Qualities:	Quirks:	Saving Grace:

NOTES:

AGENT OF **ANTAGONIST**		
Name:	**Age:**	
Physical Characteristics	Connection to Main Characters	Personal Motivation
Hair:		
Eyes:		
Height:		
Striking Features:		
		Evil Qualities:
	Function on behalf of Antagonist	

Distinctive Language:	Quirks:	Saving Grace:

NOTES:

LOVE INTEREST

Name: **Age:**

Physical Characteristics	Why wanted by Protagonist?	Personal Motivation
Hair:		
Eyes:		
Height:		
Striking Features:		
	Why wanted by Antagonist?	Evil Qualities:

Distinctive Language:	Quirks:	Fatal Flaws:

NOTES:

LOVE INTEREST / non-human

What is it?

Physical Characteristics	Protagonist desires what?	Its Motivation
Hair:		
Eyes:		
Height:		
Striking Features:		
	Antagonist desires what?	Qualities:

Distinctive Traits:	What's unusual about it?	Fatal flaws:

NOTES:

MAJOR SCENE CARD
Where in book? *Beginning   Middle   End*
Setting: **When?** *Day   Night*

Main Characters Involved:	Time:
	What happens?
Other Characters Involved:	
	Main Conflict:

Purpose of scene:	Objects:
Cliffhangers:	Smells:
Foreshadowing:	Tastes:
Emotional Distance:	Textures:
Overall Mood:	Sounds:

NOTES:

MINOR SCENE CARD

Where in book? *Beginning   Middle   End*
Setting: When? *Day   Night*

Main Characters Involved:	Time:
	What happens?
Other Characters Involved:	
	Main Conflict:

Purpose of scene:	Objects:
Cliffhangers:	Smells:
Foreshadowing:	Tastes:
Emotional Distance:	Textures:
Overall Mood:	Sounds:

NOTES:

PIVOTAL SCENE CARD: Inciting Event

Where in book? *Beginning*
Setting: **When?** *Day   Night*

Main Characters Involved:	Time:
	What happens?
Other Characters Involved:	
	Main Conflict:

Purpose of scene:	Objects:
	Smells:
Foreshadowing:	Tastes:
Emotional Distance:	Textures:
Overall Mood:	Sounds:

NOTES:

PIVOTAL SCENE CARD: Point of No Return	
Where in book? *Transition from Beginning to Middle*	
Setting:	When? *Day Night*
Main Characters Involved:	Time:
	What happens?
Other Characters Involved:	
	Main Conflict:

Purpose of scene:		Objects:	
Cliffhangers:		Smells:	
Foreshadowing:		Tastes:	
Emotional Distance:		Textures:	
Overall Mood:		Sounds:	

NOTES:

PIVOTAL SCENE CARD: Obstacle 1		
Where in book? *Middle*		
Setting:		When? *Day* *Night*
Main Characters Involved:	Time:	
	What happens?	
Other Characters Involved:			
	Main Conflict:	

Purpose of scene:	Objects:
Cliffhangers:	Smells:
Foreshadowing:	Tastes:
Emotional Distance:	Textures:
Overall Mood:	Sounds:

NOTES:

PIVOTAL SCENE CARD: Obstacle 2

Where in book? *Middle*
Setting: When? *Day   Night*

Main Characters Involved:	Time:
	What happens?
Other Characters Involved:	
	Main Conflict:

Purpose of scene:		Objects:	
Cliffhangers:		Smells:	
Foreshadowing:		Tastes:	
Emotional Distance:		Textures:	
Overall Mood:		Sounds:	

NOTES:

PIVOTAL SCENE CARD: Obstacle 3

Where in book? *Middle*

Setting:		**When?** *Day Night*
Main Characters Involved:	Time:	
	What happens?	
Other Characters Involved:		
	Main Conflict:	

Purpose of scene:	Objects:
Cliffhangers:	Smells:
Foreshadowing:	Tastes:
Emotional Distance:	Textures:
Overall Mood:	Sounds:

NOTES:

PIVOTAL SCENE CARD: Climax

Where in book? *End*
Setting: **When?** *Day   Night*

Main Characters Involved:	Time:
	What happens?
Other Characters Involved:	
	Main Conflict:

Purpose of scene:	Objects:
Cliffhangers:	Smells:
Foreshadowing:	Tastes:
Emotional Distance:	Textures:
Overall Mood:	Sounds:

NOTES:

www.ingramcontent.com/pod-product-compliance
Lightning Source LLC
LaVergne TN
LVHW041617070426
835507LV00008B/298